Robert Katende, voted the most influential man in all of Uganda

— *New Vision.* National Newspaper

Robert Katende named as one of Uganda's Tourism ambassadors by the Tourism State Minister, Godfrey Suubi Kiwanda.

— *New Vision,*
Uganda's Leading daily Newspaper

Robert Katende, named an African Ambassador to the Obama Foundation.

— The Obama Foundation

Robert Katende, through the programs he has initiated, is restoring hope and improving lives in Uganda in an unexpected way.

— Obama.org

The ObamaFoundation is connecting people from around the world so they can form partnerships like that of Robert Katende and Vanessa (of Freedom Cups). I am inspired by what's possible when leaders come together to have an even greater impact on the world.

— Barack Obama@BarackObama

Sharif learned the game at the SOM Chess Academy, an organization founded by Robert Katende. Katende is known as the coach of *Phiona Mutesi whose life was portrayed in the Disney movie,* Queen of Katwe. *He helps to manage nine centers around the poorest parts of Kampala, Uganda's capital. Sharif is one of many examples that chess can empower even the most underprivileged.*

– TheChessDrum.net

A KNIGHT
without a CASTLE

A Story of Resilience and Hope

ROBERT
KATENDE

Made for Grace Publishing

Made for Grace is an imprint of Made for Success Publishing
P.O. Box 1775 Issaquah, WA 98027
www.MadeForSuccessPublishing.com

Distributed by Made for Success Publishing

First Printing
Library of Congress Cataloging-in-Publication data
Katende, Robert
A Knight Without A Castle: A Story of Resilience and Hope

p. *cm.*

LCCN: 2019939283
ISBN: 978-1-64146-377-5 (PBK)
ISBN:978-1-64146-430-7 (EBK)
ISBN: 978-1-64146-459-8 (AUDIOBK)

Printed in the United States of America

For further *information contact Made* for *Success Publishing*
+14255266480 or *email service@madeforsuccess.net*

CONTENTS

FOREWORD

NOT LONG AFTER I first encountered Robert Katende, I came up with the nickname I have utilized to address him for nearly a decade since: The Fixer. Fixer is a term used to describe a native of a certain country who helps a foreigner figure out how to accomplish tasks there, often against all odds. Robert became that for me.

Uganda is not the ideal place for a reporter to schedule interviews. Ugandans simply don't organize themselves by the clock. So in 2010, when I initially met Robert and we began planning the interviews I hoped to do for a magazine article about one of his apprentices in the Katwe slum, Phiona Mutesi, I had no idea the heft of the challenge I was posing to him. Keep in mind, Robert was not a fixer, or at least he didn't know it yet. He was a missionary and a chess coach. As we scanned through my extensive interview list, Robert nodded agreeably. When it comes to patience, Job had nothing on Robert Katende.

I returned to Uganda in 2012 to expand my magazine story into a book titled *The Queen of Katwe*. I recall compiling a new list of thirty-five interviews that I needed to complete over five days, a herculean ask by American standards, next to impossible in Uganda. The last name on the list was Yoweri

Museveni, the president of Uganda, who I had included just to tease The Fixer. Robert responded by placing a call to a connection in the government.

After I returned to America, Robert and I engaged in a regular Sunday evening Skype. I would ask him to research and report back on specific details that I required to finish the manuscript and somehow he always collected the answers for the following Sunday, just in time to field even more editorial queries that had sprung up during the week. Finally, when it came time to shoot the movie *Queen of Katwe* in 2015, Disney hired Robert as a creative consultant and whenever the film's plot seemed to be straying from reality, it was The Fixer who steered it back on course.

The truth is that my original magazine story, my book, the movie and even *A Knight Without A Castle* may never have come to fruition had it not been for Robert's skill as a fixer. In September of 2010, Robert, Phiona, roughly a dozen others and I set off on a journey together from Uganda to the 2010 Chess Olympiad in Russia. We began the odyssey by flying to Nairobi, Kenya for a layover to change planes. When we arrived at our departure gate in Nairobi, everybody in our group was given a boarding pass except me. For some unexplained reason, I had been bumped to standby. There were about fifty other people on standby, many desperate to board that flight and the gate area could conservatively be described as chaotic. I knew that if I did not board that plane, I would miss the subsequent charter flight from Dubai to Russia and thus might not be able to complete my article, which was dependent on reporting at the Olympiad. I was informed that my prospects of escaping standby were slim at best.

Before Robert and the rest of our traveling party boarded without me, I noticed Robert beckoning a gate agent aside for a brief talk. I have never asked Robert what he said to that agent and I will never know if it had anything to do with what occurred shortly thereafter when that same agent improbably handed me a boarding pass. All I know is that when I stepped inside the plane, the rest of the Ugandan contingent viewed me like a ghost they had never expected to see again. Robert greeted me with a serene smile and his customary "Hello, Teem."

Because of my book's title, it is assumed that *The Queen of Katwe* is the story of Phiona. However, I have always maintained that it is really more about Robert, because without Robert Katende we would never have known Phiona Mutesi. It is the story of a fixer, but over the years, fixer has taken on a whole new meaning for me.

This remarkable book is the blueprint for how Robert Katende has, against all odds, fixed Phiona Mutesi as well as thousands and thousands of other lives, including his own.

— Tim Crothers, author of *The Queen of Katwe*

PREFACE

I WAS NOT fortunate enough to enter this world the "proper" way, as many of you reading this book may have. Mine was not the ideal family setting where a married couple brings their new bundle of joy into the world as a valued addition to the family. No, I was the fatal consequence of an illicit affair between a 14-year-old schoolgirl and a mature family man—a man who was already committed to his real family. I was denied the joy of growing up with a loving father to help me along and tell me how much he loved and cared about me. In fact, I was given a death sentence by this man's legal wife when I was only a few days old: She vowed to kill me if I ever set foot in their home.

My crime? Being sired by the husband of another woman.

I first learned of my name when I was over three years of age. My absentee mother—who abandoned me when I was only eight months old—and my unknown father never cared enough to name me at birth. This gloomy set of circumstances set the tone for the subsequent years of my childhood and early youth; years filled with unspeakable travails and unfathomable misery. I paid the price for crimes I never committed, and I hunted warthogs in the bush using crude spears. I oscillated between the city and my rural home hanging menacingly atop overloaded cargo trucks while accompanying my guardian grandmother on her several petty business trips because I was too young to be left alone. I never had the chance to live a normal life. I was doomed to fail, to suffer, to struggle, and to die. But I didn't die. Somehow, I have lived long enough to tell this story. This is not fiction. This is the true story of my life.

This book is based on true events that took place in my younger years. I have lived a three-dimensional life in which I have experienced as much adversity as I have privilege. I have also been involved in chess both as a player and as a coach. It is through chess that I learned countless lessons that parallel my life experiences; lessons that I share with you in this book. I have come to the conclusion that life and chess are inextricably intertwined. In chess, you can determine every move you play just the same way as you would in everyday life—you ultimately control the destiny of the game with each move. There is no guesswork in chess, just as there isn't in life, contrary to popular belief. All that matters on the chessboard is a planned good move.

In many ways, the game of chess contains rich metaphors for the human experience. Why? Because chess is more than just a game. It requires calculation, moves, analysis, interpretative skill, resilience and practice. Nothing is hidden on the board. Each day of my life has related closely to the moves on the chessboard.

In retrospect, I count all my life's experiences as invaluable lessons from which we can draw inspiration on becoming great, one move at a time. Life is not a smooth-sailing ship. Instead, it is a mixture of fortunes and misfortunes. The latter can make us or break us, depending on the attitude with which we approach life's tribulations. In his book *The Light and the Glory*, Peter Marshall wrote that, "When we long for life without difficulties, remind us that oaks grow strong in contrary winds and diamonds are made under pressure." It is vital to encourage the people going through adversities that there is a positive part to it as well that can only be beneficial if we draw the lessons toward the positive energy. I would neither be what I am today nor would I be doing what I do without the lessons I gained through life's adversities. Because of that, I don't see Katwe as a den of failures and desperation. I see it as a training ground for future kings and queens. It doesn't matter how many books you have read about this subject; I can assure you this one will give you a fresh perspective on life.

The book is divided into two parts. Part one presents the story of my life and the key lessons that can be drawn from it. It is part autobiographical and part inspirational. The second part is written by my research partner, Nathan Kiwere, with whom I conducted the qualitative research and interviews, and it focuses on testimonies of people that have been impacted by my story.

There is a proverb which states, "If you want to go quickly, go alone. If you want to go far, go together." I have traveled far in my life. By God's grace and with the support of friends, I have traversed through many winding roads and rough terrains. Thanking them all by name would require another book, and I would likely still, inadvertently, leave someone out. However, I would like to give special thanks to Maria Hwang, Aloysius Kyazze, Venita Gardener, Auntie

Jacent & Dez, Grandma Ailedah, Sal Ferlise, Karl & Camen Reese, John Carls, Tendo Nagenda, Beatriz Marinello, Pastor Nabulerere, Jason Yip, John B Third, Genie and Rich, Clenet family, Popp family, my family, the staff of Sports outreach, and all the children of SOM Chess Academy.

I dedicate this book to my wife, Sarah Katende, and our three daughters Mercy, Hope, and Grace. Every day, you teach me the value of unconditional love. You are the light of my life, the strength in my fight, the stand in my feet. You make me a better man. I dedicate it to all the stakeholders of SOM Chess Academy and The Robert Katende Initiative, not forgetting all the people involved in my vision and mission of transforming lives through chess, one move at a time

I am also dedicating this book to all who will read it and take action to better the lives of those around them by being a blessing to them.

"*Everyone has a seed of excellence that needs to be nurtured to harness their God-given abilities.*"

– Robert Katende

"*I don't think that we're meant to understand it all the time. I think that sometimes we just have to have faith.*"

– Nicholas Sparks

CHAPTER ONE
PREPARATION FOR SERVICE

PREPARATION IS VERY critical in all dimensions of life. Take the example of flying. It is almost traditional in some countries for passengers to clap after a smooth and safe landing as an expression of gratitude to the pilot for a job "well done." But what passengers don't realize is that the pilot's performance is predicated on proper preparation prior to the flight. Aviation experts aver that sometimes pilots take much longer to prepare for the flight than the actual duration of the flight. Whether the flight is 40 minutes or 8 hours long, the procedures are the same—medical check, flight data analysis, briefing, and aircraft check. Under no circumstances can the crew skip any of these steps.

The medical check is set to confirm that all cockpit and cabin crew members are mentally and physically fit to perform their duties. Usually, this includes a blood pressure check and a general examination. Should the doctor doubt the health condition of the pilot, additional tests may be conducted, including a blood test. Then, upon successful completion of the medical check, the crew starts the flight examination. The captain receives the flight data, which includes the route map, landing chart, weather forecast, etc. Along with the first officer, the captain calculates the necessary amount of fuel, depending on the aircraft load.

All this is done to ensure a safe flight that is devoid of problems. It is no wonder flying remains the safest means of transportation. Statistics indicate that as much as 99 percent of all aviation accidents are due to pilot error as opposed to aircraft malfunction. This points to pilots who overlook specific details at the preparation phase, which result in emergencies that they are unable to deal with mid-air. It also draws parallels with road transportation—the riskiest of all modes. This is because automobile drivers undertake the least preparation before settling in the driver's seat—certainly much less than that of their pilot colleagues—hence, the unrivaled tendency toward fatalities on the road. How we prepare ourselves at every stage of growth significantly impacts the nature of life that we lead. I consider the hardships I went through in my infancy and early youth as preparation for what I am today. I needed to be equipped in order to face the challenges and seek solutions for the folks I regularly encounter.

Getting here was not an easy journey. My life's journey has been one typified by perseverance, enduring faith, hope against all hope, patience, humility, forgiveness, self-control, and a host of other values that have come to define the very purpose of my existence. Most importantly, it is a testament to the resilience of the human spirit; to the truth that anyone and everyone can transcend the most harrowing experiences of life and still find true meaning for living. It is possible.

If only humanity mastered the right thing to do in the moments when you feel like you are on life-support in the world's intensive care unit; when you have been written off by all and find yourself waiting for the inevitable to happen. Even here, you still can claw yourself out of the pit of despair and make it to the finish line, not as a passive participant but as a victor. On the other hand, I have also learned that losing is not the worst thing that can happen to you. Sometimes you need to lose in order to learn something. I trust that this story casts a ray of hope upon all who think that all is lost; on those who might eventually go through what I did, or perhaps even worse.

This story is really not about inventing anything new. The Lord Jesus Christ frequently used parables as a means of illustrating profound, divine truths. Stories such as these are easily

Chess Strategy: Gain Advantage

Play for the advantage. If you already have it, maintain it. If you don't have it, seek it.

Life Lesson: Find the Silver Lining

While difficult times can feel like a deep, dark hole that we can't escape, and we often wonder "Why is this happening to me?", there is always a silver lining. It's through the difficult times in our life that we are able to grow. It's when we are tested that we are able to rise, push through and come out the other side stronger, braver, and better.

Food for Thought:

1. Set a vision
2. Map out your options
3. Think ahead
4. Devise a plan

"Mishaps are like knives that either serve us or cut us, as we grasp them by the blade or by the handle."

– James Russell Lowell

remembered—the characters bold and the symbolism rich in meaning. Before a certain point in his ministry, Jesus had employed many graphic analogies using common things that would be familiar to everyone (salt, bread, sheep, etc.), and their meaning was reasonably clear in the context of His teaching. By the same token, sharing my life has been very pivotal in helping the disadvantaged children I serve to understand that anyone can emerge from any kind of situation, and even help others out through the process. That is the reason why it is crucial for every one of us to become what we wish to teach.

The Unpleasant Welcome

My birth was indeed a very unpleasant welcome into life. Having come into the world the way I did, rejection was part of my daily existence right from the outset. It was clear that I was an unwanted child; my teenage mum, Firidah Nawaguma, was not ready to bring me into the world, and the father I never met—whose name I never knew—didn't intend to sire me. That was never his plan, at least. I was simply an inconvenient truth to him, just as I was a disruption to my mother's education and young life. It was no surprise that I was declared persona non grata in my father's house at the pain of death, if my mother dared to take me there. My mother conveniently weaned me off her breast at the time I needed it most (I am not even sure if she breastfed me at all) when she got an opportunity to start again in life—this time with a new man who had a stable income. She couldn't wait for me to make it to at least one year before running off to her newfound love. Neither could she think about letting me tag along with her to the new marital home for fear of spoiling her chances. I was expendable to her; I had no value to the people responsible for me. I was like condemned goods that are not worthy of human consumption, and I was avoided like the plague by those who were duty-bound to defend me against all odds. How I wish the laws that address child-neglect were in place at the time, perhaps this wouldn't have happened.

There were no easy options for my young mother other than putting me under the care of her sixty-year-old mother, Aidah Namusisi. Looking back, I highly doubt she thought I would pull through and make it to adulthood under the circumstances. My grandmother had no reliable income worth talking about, other than what she earned by selling bananas from her small garden; but it was just enough to feed me and my other bastard cousin brother, Kiddu. I am not sure how she managed to buy milk to feed me after the premature departure of my mother, and who knows what I grew up eating during that time. I was probably following a fully-fledged adult diet at eight months. Anything was possible during my childhood, it seems. This made life challenging right from the beginning. However, it was a childhood that eventually turned out to be a training platform and a process of self-discovery as I wandered about with my grandma—in her late 90s as of the writing of this book.

Life was more of a chaotic mess in the jungle, with survival not guaranteed. Mine was a collage of contradictions that I was too young to fathom. But it was also one that engendered a kind of early awareness about the adult world and how to deal with any situation. There is a way, it seems, in which hardships awaken our survival instinct and enable us to mount the pedestal of our self-preservation. This was key in the manner in which I encountered life in the subsequent years, as you will notice.

We never really had a permanent address we could call home. Instead, we led a kind of nomadic lifestyle, constantly wandering in search of food. We possessed nothing, not even a chicken. Grandma once rented a small shack in Kiboga town, but her failure to keep up with the bills soon forced her to return to her home village in Kiwanda Kirangira. Luckily, she had inherited a portion of land from her family that we could live off. She built a single-room mud and wattle hut to give us shelter and tilled the land so we could grow crops. Several of her relatives were in the neighborhood, giving us a sense of community. This assurance somewhat alleviated our circumstances for the time being while my creative grandma hatched alternative plans for survival.

Before we could warm up the place, circumstances conspired against us once again. Suddenly, our lives were at stake with a high risk of death. Our transition coincided with the time when rebel forces led by Yoweri Museveni were waging a guerilla insurrection against the president at the time, Apollo Milton Obote. The flashpoint of this insurgency was the infamous Luwero Triangle. Kiboga is within the precincts of this triangle; thus, we were quite literally sandwiched between a rock and a hard place! The opposing forces attacked from opposite directions while we were caught in the middle with no idea where to run.

On one occasion, however, we found ourselves in the rebel territory, where it turned out they were the more benevolent side that cared about our survival. They would inform us which places were safe to hide in and provided us advance notice as to where government soldiers intended to strike next. We came face to face with death on a daily basis as we alternated between one village and another on the advice of the rebels. Finding residents of the villages dead became the norm rather than the exception. Death stared us in the face, and we knew that it was just a matter of time before our day came. The situation was dire. Food was never a priority at that time, as Grandma had to carry Kiddu (her other grandson) and me while walking tens of kilometers, seeking safety. Years of struggle had finally taken its toll, making her body frail and spirit weary.

It was only by miracle that we made it out of the jaws of death when the rebel forces declared victory, ending the war on January 26, 1986. Surviving this war left me with a particular understanding. It was a sign that I could make it through whatever situations awaited me. The

Chess Strategy: Plan Carefully

In chess, you have to map out your options and think ahead rather than limiting your thoughts to the immediate situation. That calls for careful planning in anticipation of the future.

Life Lesson: Thoughtful Planning

To quote Lauren Hill, *"It could all be so simple, but we rather make it hard..."* Nothing is ever as bad as it seems. When you hit a roadblock, all you really need to do is focus on the next positive step. Sometimes you just need to slow down and stay calm in order to see that the answers are right in front of you.

Food for Thought:

1. Consider and weigh your options
2. Form alliances
3. Develop flexibility

"Strength does not come from winning. Your struggles develop your strengths. When you go through hardships and decide not to surrender, that is strength."

– Arnold Schwarzenegger

war had claimed several able-bodied men and women who could have escaped it quite easily. But they didn't.

Grandma had to tend to me and Julius Kiddu. Julius, who was almost my age, was a son of the elder child of my Grandma. Kiddu and I were still kids who could hardly run without an adult's support, carried on either side by an old Grandma for days, who lived to see the day of triumph without so much as a bruise from a bullet shell.

It would be too much to attribute this to Grandma alone. Looking back, it is clear to me that my Creator had plans for me. He was prepping me in anticipation of a mission I had to fulfill in the future; one that would require experience and not mere theoretical answers. Just as apostle Paul wrote to the Corinthians that, "He comforts us in all our tribulation, that we may be able to comfort them who are in any trouble, by the comfort with which we ourselves are comforted of God." (2 Cor.1.4 KJV)

My mother gave birth to four more children with her second and third husbands, whom I got a chance to meet and occasionally stay with. She lived not very far from where I stayed with Grandma, but for the protection of her marriages, we never got to bond as mother and son. Our first reunion happened when I was about four years old, immediately after the end of the war. She didn't even recognize me at the first meeting as she hurried past Grandma and me on our way to get registered by the government as returnees from the war; she only recognized her mother and then realized that I must be the one—her son. It was at that moment that she addressed me by my first name for the first time in my life.

I was still too young to understand fully, but it must have baffled me.

So now I also had a second name, just like other people I had met. Robert Katende was my full name—how liberating! Although I had nothing of my own, at least I now owned a name. Grandma only knew me as Katende, and after four years, she finally learned that my full name was Robert Katende. It is encouraging to look back and know that something everyone else takes for granted—something as seemingly small as a first name—was a gift that I deeply treasured.

Since I had not grown up with my mother, there was no initial chemistry between us at first sight. How could it be there? She had left me in the dark, where I couldn't see at all. How could I recall her face when she didn't even recognize mine? How was I to deal with this? In any case, she returned to the comfort of her other family just moments after our meeting, and I was not to see her again except on rare occasions. I must assume that she had to hide in order to meet me, as this could jeopardize her relationship with her man.

Although the war was over, we still had many things to grapple with. Grandma had to be very creative to keep food on the table. We had to make trips to the city to sell food to earn a living. Occasionally, I was called upon by some adults in the village to go on hunting expeditions for game meat. Our prey was mainly warthogs, although sporadically other wild animals came into the mix. My role (and that of other kids involved) was to scream at the top of our lungs to scare the prey and lead it to the traps. I was given a small spear for my protection, just in case the tables turned on us. Of course, it was for formality. I don't think I was in any position to defend myself in the event that the wild animal was serious enough to attack. I didn't have any form of training in hunting and self-defense. I don't even remember what sort of payment I received from the adult hunters for my services. At the most, it could have been a morsel of warthog meat, if anything at all.

It turns out things were not as rosy with my mother's family. My mother left her man as unceremoniously as she had left me years back. Perhaps they had some irreconcilable differences, as I usually hear about people who divorce these days. The truth is, I will never know. But she left him and joined us, bringing along her four other children. I had to learn to love her and my younger stepsiblings, in spite of everything. She was still my mother, and thankfully I was too young to reason things out or to choose to hate her for what she had done. I was simply relieved that there was a new ray of light at the end of the tunnel. It was the first major turning point in my life.

She soon enrolled me in primary school in Kampala. This was to be my first encounter with the civilized world. The prospect of being able to learn to read and write was a stark contrast to the rustic lifestyle of survival of the fittest. We settled in Kampala's Nankulabye slums, where we defaulted rent several times and ended up getting evicted. This forced us to relocate back and forth between the Kiwunya and Kiyaye slums. My grandma and my mother did petty trade together. It was time to flip a fresh page and look at the other side of life. I still had a mountain to climb to free my mind of the baggage of past misfortunes and lay it bare for new beginnings, but I knew it was time to unearth and unleash my full potential and become whatever I dreamed of being.

In case I thought that life had finally reverted to normal with the return of my mother, I was gravely mistaken. The honeymoon phase did not last long before tragedy struck yet again. My mother contracted a strange and deadly disease that brought her to her knees in a short time. We would soon find out that she had terminal breast cancer. My grandma abandoned her business and sat by her daughter's bedside as the doctors did as much as they could since we didn't have the means to pay the medical bills. Even though little was discussed in my presence, some of the conversations I heard from my grandma convinced me that if we had the money to pay for the medical bills, then something could have been done to salvage my mother's life. My mother, however, knew that she would never make it. She also had nothing to bequeath to me or her other children. At least my step-siblings could return to their fathers to take care of them. As for me, this was yet another doomsday unfolding before my eyes. There was nothing in her inheritance. She didn't even write a will—nothing would make the list. The only thing she did for me that would guarantee my future was to beg her cousin Jacent, who had a seemingly stable income, to take care of me in her absence.

Jacent agreed.

If that final deathbed meeting had not happened, or if Auntie Jacent had not heeded to my mother's plea, only God knows where I would be at this time. As fate would have it, she breathed her last right after they spoke. I was dealt the final blow. In chess lingua, the demise of mummy only compared with the loss of a queen at the start of the game—the queen is the most powerful piece on the chessboard.

After my mother's burial, my step-siblings were taken up by their fathers. I was alone once again, and my spirit was broken. I grieved, I mourned, and I felt that I had reached the end of my rope. How could life be so unfair? It felt like the whole world was in some kind of conspiracy against me; determined to relieve me of everything that I held so dear. Her death pushed me to the limits, until I decided that suicide was my best option. The only challenge with this option is that it cost money—money that I didn't have. The cheapest form of suicide at that time was taking rat poison. I tried to raise funds to purchase it at a nearby shop, but the shopkeeper could not hand it to me because the money was short by a few shillings. My self-proclaimed death sentence was aborted because of lack of funds. This enabled me to see the following day, as well as some happy moments after the fact that would make me appreciate having not taken my life.

I was always engaged in my routine—a combination of school and hard labor at Jacent's home. During holidays, all the kids under the care of Auntie Jacent, including me, worked hard to produce the food that the family survived on. Somehow, I slowly overcame my past and began to see the positive side of things. I was excelling in my studies and sports in equal measure, becoming the darling of many schools and their administration because of football (soccer in the U.S.). The light at the end of the tunnel was slowly starting to glimmer again after all.

No matter who you are or what you do, you will need a certain measure of preparation for the tasks that you hope to accomplish in life. We prepare well when we expect important guests at home. We prepare for job interviews, before we go for romantic dates, for travel, for childbirth … the list goes on. By the same token, we should never be deluded by thinking that our all-important purpose in life can be approached casually. We must be prepared. Remember the words of Howard Huff, "It was not raining when Noah built the ark."

As mentioned earlier, I believe that the mishaps that characterized my growing up were preparing me to deal with similar and even worse situations and to use my practical examples to give hope to those who are going through life's difficulties. I don't know what you might be facing now that is causing you stress and depression. You may be wondering how you can get out of such a situation. Some tend to quit, but remember the saying: "Quitters never win, and winners never quit." I advise, endure the hardship and seek for

Chess Strategy: Win, Draw, Learn

In chess, we win, draw, or learn. Most learning comes from unpleasant experiences. Choose to seek the positive out of each experience—losing is simply an opportunity to learn.

Life Lesson: Celebrate Life

"Why is it that we must suffer the loss of something so dear before we realize what a treasure we had? Why must the sun be darkened before we feel how genuinely impossible it is to live without its warmth? Why within the misery of absence does love grow by such bounds? Why must life be this way? It is a strange existence where such suffering makes us far better people."

– Richelle E. Goodrich

Food for Thought:

Learn to value whatever you have and celebrate life one day at a time.

the lessons from such an experience. It could be perseverance or even tolerance. It may be unpleasant, but there are lessons that can be leaned to prepare you for greatness. What doesn't break you, makes you!

"There is no harm in hoping for the best as long as you're prepared for the worst."

– Stephen King

"Challenge and adversity are meant to help you know who you are. Storms hit your weakness but unlock your true strength."

– Roy T. Bennett

CHAPTER TWO

UNLOCKING YOUR POTENTIAL

THE BIBLE TELLS us that, "Whatever your hand finds to do, do it with all your might; for there is no work, no device, nor knowledge, nor wisdom, in the grave, where you go." (Ecclesiastes 9:10, KJV)

After my mother's death, I opened my heart and prepared my mind and body to learn everything I thought would benefit my life, despite the circumstances I was going through. I was always searching for a lesson in every situation that I encountered, whether good or bad. I couldn't take anything for granted, knowing full well that the chance I had at education was never certain. When I encountered those whom I perceived to be better than me at whatever the task was at hand, I devised means to connect with them and learn from them. This kind of attitude changed the way I respond to situations. To those closest to me, this behavior was perceived as a hard work ethic; however, on the other hand, I was nicknamed a "fixer" for the way I attempted to solve everyone's problems.

One of the keys to my personal advancement was to develop a stream of inspiration within me. Self-belief is fundamental to anyone's development. It sustains you in those situations when you are burning up from within; when you cannot help but show your inward frustration, but no one comes to your rescue. You know those moments when everyone seems to have given up on you; when there is no shoulder left to lean on. The moments when it feels like no one believes in you. We all find ourselves in such situations at some point in our lives. Moments of loneliness will come for any soul that inhabits this earth, no matter where you live or what you do. I have found myself in hopeless situations like these more times than I can count; moments when I wondered what to do next. What helped me through those times when no one was there was the belief that I could learn from any circumstance that was handed to me.

Don't get me wrong; I believe that everyone needs an encourager. However, I have found myself in many situations where I needed to become my own encourager. This is the most important tool that energizes me and stirs up great ideas! It is also a source of solace during my darkest hours. I have come to realize that self-encouragement is often what enables ordinary people to do extraordinary things.

In most cases, you are likely to attract encouragement when those around you sense audacity within you. But what happens when nobody recognizes it? You strive and give your best but are rewarded with evil intentions and bad fortune. You search for a place of belonging, and it is nowhere to be found. The first unit anyone identifies with is a family. I didn't have one—no mother, no father, neither a brother nor a sister. I remember coming to a point where I was identifying with signposts that bore my name, even though I had no connection whatsoever to their context.

I experienced my mother's affection and tender loving care for no more than two years, and while I was just learning to warm up to it, she passed on in 1990. I felt my world crumble like a house of cards. A huge cloud of darkness enveloped my life, and nothing made sense anymore. It was by far the most troubling moment of my young life. I wept helplessly. I felt trapped and wondered where I could locate my next safe square on the chessboard of life.

Being the young man that I was, I was clueless. Stuck at the crossroads and unable to decide which way to go. Full of sorrow, I started to slowly figure out what to do next. I had to figure it out. There was no one else on whom I could rely. I had to fight and fill in the missing links to whatever remained of my life's puzzle. The only plausible option at that time

Chess Strategy: Be Mindful of an Opponent's Moves

Ignore what your opponent is trying to do at your own peril. We often get so absorbed in our own games and machinations that we ignore what is going on around us. Be aware of threats and alert to opportunities.

Life Lesson: Persevere

Perseverance is a virtue. We may never be able to control the circumstances around us; however, we *can* control how we respond to circumstances.

Food for Thought:

1. Remain hopeful
2. Stay positive
3. Focus on your goal
4. Practice, practice, practice

"Do not let the memories of your past limit the potential of your future. There are no limits to what you can achieve on your journey through life, except in your mind."

– Roy T. Bennett

was to go back and stay with Grandma in her rural village in Kiwanda. But that meant no more school.

I was not aware then that my mother had discussed some arrangements for me with her friend, Auntie Jacent, shortly before her death. It was after the burial that Auntie Jacent made it public to the mourners.

"Before our sister died, she talked to me about her children and revealed to me that Robert had a special place in her heart and she was very much concerned about him," she reported. "Unlike his stepsiblings, Robert has no father to take him up. She was really worried about how he would make it in life."

This revelation only served to accentuate my sorrow and made me grieve that much more. If I thought that my situation was bad before, this reminded me that things were far worse than I assumed. I continued sobbing, never even hearing the last part of the report. People tried hard to console and calm me down, but it all weighed incredibly heavily on me. I was simply too devastated at that time. I was later told that at the end of Auntie Jacent's speech, she pledged to take me to her home to stay with her for some time. Eventually, I would go and stay with other aunties as well.

It was a precious offer coming to a desperate kid who knew nothing about where his auntie even stayed. I couldn't help but get down on my knees and thank her. I realized that all my other siblings were either with their fathers or relatives from the fathers' side. That same evening, they all left as I remained behind to go with Auntie Jacent. All this only served to heighten the pain that was still boiling deep down in my heart. I was not sure whether we would ever get to see each other again. All I got to see was my entire family getting split because of the departure of the one figure that united us. I was particularly hurt to see baby Ali Tebusweke taken away by his paternal aunties; he was only eight months old at the time. I wondered whether he would ever make it to adulthood. Those memories remained with me for some time; mental images that bled with despair and hopelessness.

Henry Kirugga, Esseza Nabuule, Sam Buule, and Annet Nagadya all left with their dad, James Kiwanuka. James was a civil servant staying in Kibuli senior quarters, a suburb in Kampala city not far from Kibuli slums, where I now have a Chess Academy center. Although I had visited their home before, I wasn't confident I would ever get to see them again. I didn't even know where I was to be taken!

The day after my mother's burial, I also bid farewell to Grandma as the time came to leave with Auntie Jacent. I followed like a goat without questioning anything, but at the same time, tried to memorize every corner and turn we took on the way until I could no longer remember. Auntie Jacent had a good house with a fence, electricity, and running water. We arrived in the night, and I was led straight to the living room. It was the nicest-looking place that I had ever seen or set my foot in. I sank into the comfy couch that lay opposite the big color Hitachi television set with sides of brown wood and three big knobs in the front. The wall was filled with nicely framed family photographs on one side and a big hand-painted picture of the family head, Haji Amir Kasolo, on the other side. Despite the temptation, I tried to take in the beauty without touching a thing, attempting to act as though I was already familiar with the surroundings. I kept a bold posture so no one would notice my anxiety.

Soon it was time for dinner, and I was served matooke (steamed mashed bananas) with spiced beef stew. I noticed some strange spices in the soup and ate while sorting them aside on my plate. One of the kids took note and raised it among the group. "This boy doesn't eat carrots," she observed. Apparently, the strange orange things I had sorted out were called carrots. I quickly realized there were many new things that I had to learn in this unfamiliar territory, not to mention the additional challenge of the kids of the house being very quick to detect and point out my peculiarities. Their taunting words caused me constant embarrassment and created the impression that I was an uncivilized village boy.

It took me a while to get used to the new place. I couldn't hide my learned mannerisms—clearly, the place was above my station. Thankfully, the harsh treatment gave way to a few sympathies from some of the children at the home. In order to fit in, I had to make several adjustments that were not easy at all. I had to unlearn years of rural customs. My bush lifestyle in Kiboga and the Nakulabye ghetto attitude had not prepared me for urban ways. What had taken years to learn would surely not change in a matter of days. It took time.

There was one girl in the house who shared a name with Auntie Jacent. She stood out in the fact that she was constantly inflicting cruelty on me without any reason. She was the highly favored girl among all supported children, and she was particularly loved by Auntie Jacent. She was one of the children of a late uncle. She really made my stay in the home very unpleasant—so much so that I started to develop consistent suicidal thoughts. She was older than me and already in secondary school. It seems my coming in the home, and perhaps my hardworking ways, threatened her position as the most favored. She derived pleasure in taunting and tormenting me at every opportunity, perhaps to assert her place in the house but also to remind me about my own.

Finding education was the best thing that ever happened to me. Suddenly, I was cast on the same plane of opportunity as everyone else. Once I liberated my mind from the past, it was not difficult for me to start to bring to the surface the gifts that God had deposited in me. In any case, erasing my history was certainly not going to be a walk in the park. Growing up in rural Kiboga meant that I had no grasp of the English language, unlike my colleagues, many of whom grew up speaking it as a second language. My language command was limited to Luganda, and that meant the first years in my new school were not going to be easy. I struggled to master English, the only language that was used in teaching all the subjects. It was my sheer determination that helped me to find the confidence to join the race despite being so disadvantaged. This determination would later see me through many adversities and lead me to scale heights while others faced defeat.

I am reminded here of the scripture, "I returned, and saw under the sun, that the race is not to the swift, nor the battle to the strong, neither yet bread to the wise, nor yet riches to men of understanding, nor yet favor to men of skill; but time and chance happens to them all." (Ecclesiastes 9:11, KJV) One doesn't have to be a practicing Christian in order to appreciate the significance of this statement. In my mind,

I could easily have disqualified myself as the "unwashed" underdog from the rural setting or the ghetto, here to compete with the more refined city-born kids whose mannerisms were at odds with my own. But God had bigger plans. Besides English, I had many social things to learn, including wearing shoes. Strange as it might sound, I had never had the opportunity to own a pair of shoes before. I had to start with flip flops, and this did not come without inconvenience. The strap that passed between my big toe and the next one was too much for me to bear. It caused severe discomfort for a while before I got used to it. With the kind of primitivity that engulfed me, I knew quite well what I was up against.

Nevertheless, I chose to single-mindedly focus my attention on what mattered most and ignore the rest. All this notwithstanding, I was confident that we all had an equal shot in life and that much was immaterial in the race to the finish line. I discovered that I was good at numbers. I also discovered my competitive nature and began to train in football.

What is the Purpose of Your Life?

Discovering your potential is, in a way, inextricably interwoven with understanding your purpose in life. It is very likely that as you read this book, you have wondered at one time or another why you exist. So, you will ask: what is my purpose? Is there even a purpose in life? If there is, what is it?

This question has been asked by every sane person who has walked this earth. It can be quite a disturbing question, particularly if the answers are elusive. Moreover, it is one to which answers have to be found, if life is to ever make sense. So then, where do we find our purpose in life? Who determines it? Anyone with the right attitude and resolve can rise to the occasion and reinvent him or herself. In the *Seven Habits of Highly Effective People*, Steven Covey states that "Anyone can become the second creation of his own proactive design." This statement relates to the notion that following all the major early life influences that one can possibly go through, such as those depicted earlier in this book about my own early life, it is still possible to make a conscious decision about like. One can retract from all illusions and orientations sponsored by forces external to one's personality and find a new ideological alignment that is consistent with one's personal vision of the world.

I was able to discover my potential in spite of (and also because of) the challenges that I contended with early in life. I learned many lessons that now resonate with my values and beliefs. For instance, I now understand potential as a treasure in everyone; stored in a locked metallic box within an individual. The ability to realize what you are capable of being or becoming sets you on the journey to determine the four W's and H: What, where, when, who and how.

Who am I? What can I do? Where can I do it? When should I do it? How should I do it?

These are critical questions that all of us must answer at some point in our lives.

The pursuit of my potential was not some kind of accidental occurrence; it was and has always been a deliberate action that I daily work toward developing to its fullness. I aim at realizing what I believe I am capable of being or doing irrespective of where I am or what I am going through. I call it a metallic box because you have to intentionally use more effort to get to your full potential. The willingness to make myself more useful and resourceful enabled me to discover the power within me and create a difference in my life (and now in the lives of others).

Yielding a character of excellence in my endeavors is one of the determining factors in creating the difference. I have learned to perceive some of the negative aspects of life in a positive light. Sometimes when I FAIL (First Attempt In Learning), I don't despair because failure sets me back to the drawing board to devise other possible ways. I have trained myself to take the FAIL as a First Attempt in Learning; NO as there will be a Next Opportunity, and the feeling of coming to an END as Effort Never Dies. I now use these inspirations to press on towards the goal set before me.

We could learn a lot from the famous example of Michael Jordan, the best basketball player in NBA history. His life testifies about failure. One time, when interviewed by a reporter about why he was successful, he said, "I have failed over and over and over in my life; that's why I succeed." What a fantastic attitude towards failure. Not many people have the patience to try out something more than a handful of times. The majority quit after trying once or twice. If Jordan had not persisted with his training and trials, he would not have landed in the basketball record books as a legend. If Lewis Howard Latimer and Thomas Edison had given up on their preliminary light bulb experiments, we might not have ever seen the invention come to pass. To them, each failure was simply another stepping stone to the next stage of development. Great success is built on failure, frustration, and even catastrophe. Albert Einstein did not speak until he was four years

Chess Strategy: Winning the War

If you spend all of your time chasing lowly pawns, you may be on the receiving end of an opponent who cares less about small victories and more about winning the war.

Life Lesson: Find Purpose

"The greatest tragedy in the world is not death, but living life without a purpose."

- Myles Munroe

Food for Thought:

The world can be a very dark place sometimes, but when you understand how to play to your advantage, identify your options and seize the opportunities available to you, you will always be two steps ahead from the rest of the pack.

"Many of life's failures are people who did not realize how close they were to success when they gave up."

- Thomas A. Edison

old and did not read until he was seven. He turned out to be one of the most celebrated scientists of all time.

I recall playing football as a child, using only my right leg to kick the ball until I met a boy named Andrew in our neighborhood. Andrew knew how to kick the ball well using both legs. This challenged me a great deal. I wondered how he was able to do that! The following day I was playing on his team, and I would pass every ball I received to him. This endeared me to him; he began to like me. I asked him to teach me how to kick the ball using my left leg as well. I remember in my first lesson, I kicked my right leg instead of the ball, and I landed on the ground. I actually sustained an injury, and, for the entire week, I was unable to play, although I kept on going back to watch the others. During this break, I was able to watch him closely and learn how to swing the leg while kicking the ball with the left. When I resumed playing, it became easy for me to master the technique and retain my balance at the same time.

I remember in the few days that followed I was able to score my first goal using the left leg. It was a reasonable shot at the goal, and the goalkeeper couldn't stop it. I was very excited. I celebrated and immediately dashed to Grandma to tell her how I had scored using my left leg. From her response, I noticed this was of little consequence, and she was not really amused at such a rather "flimsy" achievement. I didn't share her sentiments. I continued to celebrate my little victories because they encouraged me to press on. These small achievements gave me assurance that I was also capable of making it. These were my happy moments that were occasioned by my personal initiatives and not from external forces. I felt like I owed it to myself to be happy—that my happiness was *my* responsibility. I couldn't wait around for others to give happiness to me. My play area was a stone's throw from Grandma's place. It was easy for me to run back and forth between home and the play area to celebrate a goal on and off pitch. Through more practice, my left foot became equally strong and reliable and soon I could use either foot with ease.

I believe there are moments in life when you need to motivate yourself instead of waiting for someone else to do it for you. Grandma's indifference to my little achievement of learning to shoot with the left leg prepared me for many other situations that I would encounter later in life, times when I would need to lift myself up, moments when I did so much and yet received nothing in appreciation or was even paid back with scorn. Those times were sure to come, and God knew that He would have to find me already grounded on a firm foundation.

Playing football at school established me as a young luminary among students and the school administration. My sporting skills earned me a big fan base, more so due to my prolific goal-scoring with both feet. Despite being pint-sized and young, I was constantly selected by the bigger students to play on their teams. This gave me more confidence. Throughout my school years, I was popular among the entire school community. The many friends I earned also helped me in times of need. I respected everyone and worked hard in my studies. I was quite good at calculus, but somehow found the English language challenging. The first sentence I constructed was when I was requesting a teammate to pass the ball to me.

I shouted: "Beat here, beat here…" Such was the ineptitude that dogged my mastery of English, leaving me always afraid to open my mouth and speak for fear of being made fun of.

Among my many friends were children who were better than me in academics. Because we were friends, they would help me with the subject matter I found difficult to grasp. I always made a deliberate effort to improve myself and eventually score better than those who had helped me. Often this cost me some friends as I set the bar high for them, even though they were initially the people helping me. Some of them didn't like the fact that I was always catching up and sometimes surpassing them. But I had to learn to deal with that, too. More importantly to me, discovering my nascent abilities was a constant reminder that there was something intrinsic in me that could turn my situation around, if only I knew what it was and worked hard at it.

First, I discovered football while using my right foot and soon I learned to use both feet. This helped me to score goals that earned me friends and other attendant benefits. I didn't think that my abilities were limited to football. There had to be something else hidden within that could add to my potential and ultimately to my welfare.

The question is, what was that?

Our Creator placed within us inherently potent mental and physical resources to subdue the universe. That is what God told the first man, Adam: "…multiply and subdue the world." God could not have given such a command to Adam if He did not believe that Adam was capable of dominating the creation. When automobile builders put a speedometer reading 240 kilometers per hour, it means they have built in a mechanism that supports that speed range, and thus, the vehicle has the capacity to perform to that speed without a hassle. It also means that every single component of that automobile has been designed to support this cruise ability without getting affected by the external factors. However, rarely do drivers test their cars at anywhere near the speed limit. In fact, some of them fear that the car could be ruined from "over speeding." So, they prefer to play it safe by driving within the "reasonable" range, ostensibly to save the car from damage. This mentality is also alive among some people who think self-preservation is a virtue that they should live with.

Unfortunately, self-preservation does not apply when it comes to maximizing potential; it only serves to limit you from reaching your full speed.

"Hold yourself responsible for a higher standard than anybody else expects of you. Never excuse yourself. Never pity yourself. Be a hard master to yourself and be lenient to everybody else."

– Henry Ward Beecher

"*Some of the reasons you gave up were not because it was hard, but because you didn't know you were winning.*"

— ANONYMOUS

CHAPTER THREE

ALWAYS LOOK AT THE POSITIVE

IMAGINE THIS: YOU'RE about to make your game-ending move, when out of nowhere, your opponent puts you in check. All chess players understand that instead of crumbling under the stress of your plan having gone awry, being flexible allows you to quickly rework your options and continue with the game. Could this same technique be applied in everyday life?

When it comes to your career, parenting, or your relationships, even the best-laid plans don't always pan out. Being flexible allows you to adapt under constantly changing circumstances and strengthens your ability to think on your feet. Flexibility can be achieved quite easily if you maintain a good measure of positivity. Choosing to look on the bright side of things helps you to have a balanced view of adversity. Romans 8:28 says, "And we know that all things work together for good to them that love God, to them who are called according to His purpose." (KJV) I needed this kind of energy to navigate the challenges I was bound to face in the subsequent months and years of my life.

My grades at school were surprisingly quite encouraging. I completed my primary (elementary) level at St. Elizabeth Namasuba Primary school. After my final primary exit exams, I had to go to the village to continue with my routine work in the garden, which I did every weekend and during holidays. Because I worked during my time off from school, I was unable to complete the mandatory Form X required to make school selections for high school attendance. I planned to list Makerere College School as my first choice, mostly because I was captivated by the name Makerere, but also because it was located within the precincts of the prestigious and famous Makerere University. The forms were brought in the week after our final exams, at the time when I had already left for the village of Mpambire in Mpigi to work.

Throughout the entire holiday, I was roaming from one village garden to another, as Auntie Jacent required. I even went to Mubaango, the ancestral village where my mother was buried. I continued to work there under the guidance of Uncle Peter Nkuwe (RIP), who lived there with his family. Uncle Peter took me to help Kavumba Primary School in sports during the first academic term there. Schools were competing in all field events, and I was taking part in four items: both high and long jump competitions, as well as the 100m race and short relay races.

I dominated the high and long jump. As a result, I was selected to represent the region at the district level. Incidentally, it was during this time that the results for primary exit exams came back. I had passed my first national examination in first grade, and I was categorized as one of the best performers in my district. But, remember, I had missed filling in Form X; therefore, I couldn't be admitted to Makerere College School, despite having qualified.

Not being able to enroll at Makerere was heartbreaking for me, but not all was lost. Uncle Amir was thrilled with my results, and he assured me that with my performance, it would be easy to get into any other school. I continued with my garden work until the time when Aunt Jacent came with the news that Uncle Amir had gotten me a place in Lubiri Secondary School.

Did I hear her right? I thought she said Lubiri Secondary School!

Lubiri was the same school where Jacent, that "monster" girl that tormented me at home, was studying. I couldn't believe I was going to attend the same school as Jacent. I felt utterly disoriented with this development, and I spent a fair amount of time trying to devise a plan in my head on how to circumvent it. Upon receiving the admission forms, I realized that there were two different sections, whereby senior one and two attended in the afternoon, while senior three and four went for the morning shift. Ugandan education was on a double section system. This came as a massive relief to me because Jacent was in senior three. Such was the animosity between the two of us that I could not stand treading the same path to school or staying on the campus grounds at the same time.

I continued to excel academically, and I was always at the top of my class until I completed my ordinary level. My academic success was notwithstanding the 10km trek I had to make between home and school for a whopping four years from Namasuba, where I stayed with Auntie Jacent, to Lubiri Secondary School in Rubaga.

Unfortunately, the time had come when Auntie Jacent had to release me because it was getting economically challenging for her following her retirement from her bank job. None of the other aunties were willing to take me on because their husbands wouldn't allow it, so Auntie Jacent asked me to look for a place where I could stay. I approached some relatives on my father's side, hoping to take refuge there. I hadn't stayed with any of them since my childhood, so I assumed that they would feel guilty enough to do something this time. Once again, I was wrong. None of them welcomed me to stay, although they always appeared happy to see me whenever I visited. I did not know what to make of this. Was this genuine happiness, or the usual pretense that I had been served by most of my people? If indeed they were happy to see me, why then was it so hard for them to let their own blood, a lost young man, seek sanctuary in their homes at his darkest hour?

Auntie Jacent was overwhelmed with burdens and without a regular income, yet besides her own children, she had several of us from relatives to support, so she was compelled to let me go and find someone else to support me. She had played her part and fulfilled my mother's death wish for seven years. I am forever grateful to her for how far she brought me; for the sacrifices she made to accommodate me at the time when all doors had slammed shut. Now it was time to soldier on, yet things looked bleak again with nowhere to turn. The good news was that Auntie Jacent pledged to continue meeting my tuition because she could not let my good performance in school go to the dogs. However, she simply could not manage to house me under her roof anymore.

She had serious struggles with finances, made worse by the feeling that my other relatives had left the entire burden on her, even though they had agreed after the burial that they would step in—which they never did. I had also developed some vices due to the harsh treatment and torment I faced at home. I started going to play football for money, buying myself eats and other personal effects. At home, I never received like the other kids—even the things I was entitled to have. The fact that I was going out to play for money caused me to miss out on doing the chores at home. This never pleased Auntie Jacent and, to this day, I believe my lack of doing chores contributed to my eviction as well.

During my stay with Auntie Jacent, I discovered where some of my other aunties lived, as well as some of my paternal relatives. Grandma was staying in the Kasubi ghetto on the outskirts of Kampala city, where she was eking a living by selling onions in the Kasubi market. She was staying in a single ten-by-eight-foot shack with one of her grandchildren, Nagguja.

Out of desperation, I reached out to my other aunties who had pledged to support me shortly after the burial of my mother. Sadly, none of them agreed to take me on, at least at that time. I eventually ended up at Auntie Dez's place. Of all people, Auntie Dez owed my late mother and me the favor to intervene in my situation and welcome me with open hands—at least based on our culture because she is the one who inherited my mother. Unfortunately, she too turned out like everyone else. "I wouldn't have a problem bringing you in, but my husband does not support the idea, and I can't go against his word," she told me. She reminded me that she already was taking care of another boy who belonged to a relative, so her house was already full.

Next, I approached the relatives of my father, who were staying in Nateete at the time. One of them was my sister's father, and the other was his older brother. He owned a primary school in Mutundwe near Kampala city. The last time I had paid them a visit, they were incredibly excited to see me, as I was a true member of their family. I was hoping that I would receive a similar welcome and, perhaps, an invitation to stay with them. But it seems my streak of disappointments was not about to end just yet. They both gave a great measure of excuses to explain why they could not accommodate me. I felt like I had reached the end of my tether, like a starving goat roped on a post: It has exhausted all the grass within its radius and is left to stare at the abundance of food just beyond its reach. I have never felt so lost in my own land, rejected by those I thought were family. I felt so betrayed by pretentious relatives I thought were smiling with me, and yet all they exposed were poison-laden snake fangs. I was exhausted, and I felt so ill-treated.

The only trump card left in my pocket was to go to the one person who would never turn her back on me, whatever the circumstances. I gathered myself and went like a weather-beaten cock to join Grandma Namusisi in her minuscule shack in Kasubi, where she would sometimes go without food if she didn't make enough money from her onion business. Predictably, she welcomed me with open hands and tried as hard as she could to make me comfortable under the circumstances.

I told Auntie Jacent that I would go and stay with Grandma. Her husband, Uncle Amir, felt sorry that I was leaving, but he could not help it. Auntie Jacent informed me that she would be paying my tuition for that term in senior high, if I would be willing to walk from Kasubi coming from Grandma's place and go to school. Although I was pleased about the tuition, I was very much troubled about the commute.

When I left, I was given a small mattress. I put the few clothes I had in a plastic bag and said my last goodbyes to everyone at home. It was a deeply challenging situation for me, but I had to leave and live just like a refugee—except I still lived in my own country. The many football friends I had were all in their parents/guardian's homes. I don't remember sharing my struggles with any of them because all they saw of me was on the football field playing good soccer. None of them had any idea of what I was going through at home. As it had always been, football became my safe haven. Whenever I was playing, I would forget the troubling life surrounding me. Playing football made me feel alive, and I felt loved not only by my teammates but by the fans, too.

However, looking at the living status of my grandma in Kasubi in comparison to Auntie Jacent's home, it was like I was back to square one! She didn't even have a mattress. She had collected cardboard papers and formed a makeshift cushion to sleep on, so the small mattress I had been given would have to serve us both. We had to readjust the sleeping arrangement in such a small space, but we made it work. Every night, we used her garment, *gomesi,* as a bedsheet, allowing our heads and chest to rest on the mattress while the rest of our bodies rested on the cardboard papers. She had no meaningful possessions, and the shack door had no lock. Now that we had a small mattress, we had to devise a lock so that our mattress would not be stolen while we were away. It was all very depressing. I even thought about looking for some petty jobs so that I could earn some money for our survival.

However, the opportunity to have my school tuition paid was a golden opportunity. I reasoned that I could thrive in academics, which would lead to a better future for us. Nateete was much closer to Lubiri SS compared to Kasubi, which made for a tougher commute. Grandma's shack was not sturdy enough to stop the waters from coming inside whenever it rained, so it wasn't an environment conducive to study. Even so, the fighter spirit in me prompted me to try my last chance instead of yielding to rejection. With my mattress on my head and polythene bag in hand, I headed to Nateete, hoping that my father's relatives—the same that I had earlier approached—would somehow feel pity for me and change their minds and allow me to stay. Much to my dismay, I made an even bigger fool of myself instead. They became irritated by my stubborn insistence and reemphasized that their decision was final—no amount of pitiful posturing would change that. I was assured that if they had a way out, they would not have hesitated to take me on. This exchange left me in tears of disbelief, shaking my head at their cruelty.

I then embarked on my return journey to Kasubi. While I walked back to Grandma, I began to think about my options. A couple of thoughts ran through my mind, but nothing outweighed the long-term advantages of an education. When Grandma saw that I had returned, she immediately knew that, once again, I had been denied. In contrast to my other experiences, she received me with gladness and rearranged the room for my permanent stay. When I joined her, Grandma already had a granddaughter named Naggujja, who was about seven years old staying with her. So, the three of us had to determine ways of feeding ourselves, as well as paying the rent.

Grandma tried her best to put food on the table by selling onions on the street of Kasubi market. Because of her advanced age, most people knew her by name and customers would buy from her out of sympathy for her frailty. But still, her earnings were not sufficient to cover the rent and the food at home.

Shortly after settling back in with Grandma, I became more serious about both my studies and football. This time around, I had all the weekends to myself since I wasn't going to the garden. The additional free time meant that I could spend more time practicing, and also earn some money from football, playing as a mercenary (ringer in the U.S.) in different community teams. There were times when I earned enough to completely cover rent for Grandma, as well as other basic necessities like buying kerosene for the lamp I would use at night to complete school reading assignments.

All of my practicing eventually led me to be recruited for the school football team. But this did not come without risks. One evening, as we were playing a match at school, I had a brutal collision with the goalkeeper and hit the ground head first. I wound up with multiple fractures in my lower jaw and was left in a coma for over twelve hours. I was rushed to Mulago Referral Hospital. Unfortunately, Grandma was completely unaware of my whereabouts. The school reached out to Auntie Jacent because they had her address in the school books, who then reached out to Auntie Dez. She managed to make it to the hospital, and later that day brought Grandma, who would come to the hospital the subsequent days to visit me. I was in excruciating pain. A few of my classmates came to visit as well, but I couldn't utter a word because my jaws had been sealed with wires. The doctors said that I would never be able to play football again because of the risk of re-injury.

After my discharge from the hospital, Auntie Dez convinced her husband, David Galiwango, to let me recover in their home, which was located in Kibuye, within a stone's throw from the Katwe ghetto. It took me about five weeks before I had the wires removed; however, I continued to feed using a straw because I couldn't chew. Although I was getting better, it took me over four months to be able to chew

Chess Strategy: Emotions Can Dull Rational Thinking

A threat is best met with a move that improves your own position. Don't get trapped into mindlessly trading moves and material in anger. Sometimes the solution is more gentle and cerebral.

Life Lesson: Be Strategic

Strategy doesn't provide immediate answers to the problem, but it can lead to long-lasting solutions. One way to strategize is to connect with the right like-minded people.

Food for Thought:

Sometimes you get stuck in a position known as zugzwang in chess: this means no matter what move you make, you don't change the board situation but it helps you gain tempo. This is just the way it goes sometimes, both in chess and in life.

"There is always a better way; your challenge is to find it."

– ANONYMOUS

properly or open my mouth normally. I missed school for the whole term and had to wait for the second term to begin before I could restart. Unfortunately, I was about to receive more devastating news. Auntie Jacent had run out of money, and she could no longer afford to pay for my education.

The news hit me as hard as the goalkeeper had in my football collision. I had invested all my hope in getting an education. Just when I thought life was beginning to turn around, I was dealt yet another devastating blow. Things seemed to be following a familiar pattern I had experienced from childhood: Every major breakthrough would be eventually countered by an equally heartbreaking event. When I left Auntie Jacent's place to stay with Grandma in the slum, I focused on football and started earning money from it. Then my jaw injury occurred after the collision and sidelined me for about two years. Now, my tuition source was cut off. I didn't believe that this chain of events could have been sheer coincidence. However, at the time, I had no answers.

I tried to explain my predicament to the school administration, but Mr. Ssemugooma, the head teacher, told me that because this was a government school, he had no leeway to exempt anyone from paying tuition, no matter how grave the situation (I know this may sound strange to some of you with free public education systems). I desperately wrote letters to different relatives and friends asking for any sort of support, but yet again, it was all in vain.

A few days later, I was listening to a local radio station called Central Broadcasting Service (CBS), which belongs to the Buganda Kingdom. They were announcing a scholarship program supported by the Kingdom. Being a Muganda, I thought I stood a good chance to win the scholarship, and I applied. In the end, it was another flop. Such seemed to be my story at the time.

Meanwhile, I continued nursing my injuries. I realized that my steady recovery from my injuries also meant that my days at Auntie Dez's were numbered since the deal was limited to the time of recovery. Soon I would have to move back to the Kasubi slum at Grandma's, and that really worried me. I stood a better chance of receiving opportunities while staying with Auntie Dez, especially since the prospect of an education appeared to be lost. During my time at their house, I learned that Uncle David was constructing a house in Kiwanga Seeta in the Mukono district, about 20 kilometers from the city center. It was already roofed, and the windows and doors were burglar proof but had no glass. It was surrounded by a sizeable piece of land that could work well for cultivation. I saw an opportunity there and calculated in my head how much mileage I could get with a little investment of my past gardening experience. I managed to convince Auntie Dez to permit me and John, the young relative who was staying with them, us go to Mukono and cultivate some food. After all, there was a house under construction where we could sleep! After some initial hesitation, her husband agreed and there I was, happy again.

Through all of these ups and downs, I've learned that no situation is permanent. Where there is a hill, there must be a slope as well; where there is a mountain, there is also a valley, and night must be followed by dawn. They say that the darkest hour is just before dawn, and it is only in the darkness that we are able to see the stars. In looking back at all the suffering that I have endured since I was born, I can definitely see this pattern. There is not a single trial that I have ever encountered that did not eventually present a way out, whether this solution was orchestrated by me or people around me—or even circumstances beyond human control. It reminds me of the Scripture in 1 Corinthians 10:13, "No temptation has overtaken you that is not common to man. God is faithful, and he will not let you be tempted beyond your ability, but with the temptation he will also provide the way of escape, that you may be able to endure it." (ESV)

Opportunities will always present themselves, but it will be up to you to recognize them and act on them. These opportunities are everywhere; the challenge is that most times we are completely fixated on our problem, wallowing in self-pity. We are more interested in attracting sympathy than opening our eyes wider to be able to discern the opportunity presented in the challenge. These days I hear of notions like "sympathy addiction," referring to people who are in the habit of manipulating others for sympathy. I tried that when I put a mattress on my head and carried a polythene bag with my only possessions in my hand and approached my relatives in Nateete to open their doors for me… but it didn't work. It was a form of manipulation, and some people use this sort of thing habitually. Sympathy addiction also has a correlation with the defeatist mentality, which means that you give up before you've even started, like the runner who is so convinced he's going to lose the race that he doesn't even bother to go to the starting line. A defeatist is the opposite of an optimist. The solution to overcoming this pessimistic attitude is to actually take a leap of faith—take that first step that will give you the propulsion you need. Life is like a race; you either move or you get trampled.

So, as a leap of faith, John and I left for our mission in Mukono. The state in which we found the place can only compare to what is portrayed in post-apocalyptic science fiction movies. It looked like an abandoned outpost with overgrown bushes surrounding it. We had to use empty cement bags to block the gaping windows and doors that were still lacking glass. We cleared the bushes and, in less than a week, made the place habitable. We then directed our attention to the surrounding land. We tilled and planted food, including beans, cassava and corn. We worked tirelessly, only taking short breaks for lunch. After a week, we were visited by Auntie Dez and her husband. They couldn't believe their eyes. They were pleasantly surprised and pledged to supply whatever requirements we needed for our stay. Even more importantly, they were moved to finish their house. In less than three months, they had begun to fix all the glass in the windows. This was a victory for me. At least I would never have to return to Grandma's shack in the ghetto. With all that I had done to breathe new life in my Auntie's abandoned house, there was no way they were going to tell me to leave.

"In order to keep us from becoming too attached to earth, God allows us to feel a significant amount of discontent and dissatisfaction in life - longings that will never be fulfilled on this side of eternity. We're not completely happy here because we're not supposed to be here! Earth is not our final home; we were created for something much better."

– Rick Warren

Despite the doctor's report that I would never be able to play football again, I was already back at it just a few months down the road. The pain in my jaws had not completely subsided, though, and I felt it whenever I tried to juggle or head the ball. This led to prolonged headaches. I continued working out my jaws by chewing gum as doctors had suggested. Gradually the pain left as I did light training on the pitch.

Soon, I joined the community football team, and people started to notice the gift I had been given with sports. An inter-clan tournament was organized and, unsurprisingly, I was in pole position to play first team football again. I was selected to play for the *Mamba* (lungfish) clan to which my uncle David Galiwango belonged, instead of the *Lugave* (pangolin) clan to which my name belonged. The mix-up is because the local community mistook me to be Galiwango's son. The good thing was that the pangolin clan could not raise enough players to make up a team. Their absence in the tournament made it possible for me to play for the lungfish without people raising any complaints.

Playing for the lungfish clan brought more fame to the entire family of Mr. Galiwango—derived from having a talented son. This not only made me famous, but also earned me new friends and more favor from the community members. The team I represented won the tournament that year, and soon we began to play in inter-community competitions that made my name all the more renowned. We were so successful that one of my teammates called Hamis Kitagenda eventually made it to the Uganda national football team, the Cranes.

*"You don't drown by falling in water;
you drown by staying there."*

– Edwin Louis Cole

CHAPTER FOUR
CULTIVATING A SENSE OF HOPE

A YEAR AND a half had passed since I left Auntie Jacent's place. I had missed one year of school—partly because of the accident on the football pitch, but mostly because of the lack of tuition. In what was a truly surprising visit, Auntie Jacent came to Mukono and found me working in the garden. She told me to wrap up my work quickly so she could take me to a Catholic foundation at St. Matia Mulumba in Old Kampala, where she had a friend working as the secretary for the foundation. She was exploring possibilities for a scholarship for me to resume school, and this was our first step. I quickly readied myself and picked up my senior four transcripts and other academic reports.

When we arrived at St. Matia, the secretary was very impressed with my academic track record. However, she informed us that the intake for that year had already closed, and that selection of beneficiaries was always made by the Fathers and Sisters from the main Catholic Diocese. After they had made their choices clear, the selections would then have to be approved by the foundation's directors. Still, she promised to find another way. She would marshal all the balances from the children they support and forward it to me for my tuition. She made it clear that by doing so she was bending the rules because what she was opting for was off the record. She told me to check with her after a week. True to her word, she was able to collect 100,000 shillings (approximately $60). While this was a significant break-through for me, it was only sufficient to cover a fraction of the required tuition in high school at $60 a trimester. I tried several schools, but the money I had wasn't even a third of what they required.

I then decided to change the approach. Instead of start-ing with the tuition, I chose first to present my academic transcripts. That is precisely what I did when I went to Progressive Secondary School in Bweyogerere, on the out-skirts of Kampala city. I handed my papers to Mr. Mugisha, the Academic Registrar, for a place in senior five. Predictably, he was incredibly impressed by what he saw on the docu-ments. He asked me why I had not studied the previous year, and I told him about the accident on the pitch that required me to stay home for some time. He told me that my grades were outstanding, and that I had a guaranteed place in their science class. He proceeded to ask me about the combina-tion I wanted to take, when I wanted to start and whether I was joining the boarding or day section—staying at school or commuting from home, respectively. Only then did I decide to bring up my financial predicament. After breaking down the tuition for boarding and day sections for me, I told him the amount I could afford: 100,000 shillings. I explained my situation to him and why it was going to be impossible for me to join their school under their terms and conditions.

While he went to consult the school director, Mr. Kaawa Elisa Amooti, on the matter, I stayed back and prayed for God's favor upon me. The duo returned, and after asking me a few more personal questions, the director told me to pay the money I had and be enrolled in the day section. This was one of the greatest miracles of my young life! I was exceedingly grateful to both of them.

I completed the registration form for senior five as my head swirled with possibilities. Finally, a breakthrough that felt like it could last! The 6km walk back home in Kiwanga felt like 60 meters to me. The overwhelming joy I had overshadowed any fatigue from that journey as I felt that not all was lost after all. When I informed Auntie Dez about the developments, her main

Chess Strategy: Find the Best Move

In chess, every move has a purpose. A good opening prepares for a good middle game, and a good middle game prepares for a good end game. It's the reason chess players always search for the best move possible in every situation throughout the entire game.

Life Lesson: Your Responses Reflect Who You Are

Every decision changes the *game of life*. We are who we are because of the decisions we make and how we respond to circumstances that come our way, whether they are good or bad.

Food for Thought:

Life obviously cannot be lived with as much unceasing calculation as chess, nor should we want to live it that way, but there are times when we must align our actions with a predetermined strategy instead of bumbling through it.

1. Move aggressively and with purpose
2. Retreat is sometimes the best offense
3. The shadow of defeat can be the dawn of victory
4. The etiquette of resigning

"The majority sees the obstacles; the few see the objectives; history records the successes of the latter, while oblivion is the reward of the former."

- Alfred Armand Montapert

issue was the distance I had to cover daily between home and school, but I assured her that that was the least of my worries.

Within a week of getting my admission, I had started school. The majority of the students were in the boarding section; only a handful of us were in day. The school had an excellent volleyball team that occasionally took part in the national championships, but I noticed they lacked a school football team. I offered to start one with the help of the school administration. On top of that, I initiated a netball team for the girls. My role was to mobilize and coach them.

I remember how they had to use a football during practice until we lobbied the school administration to buy a proper netball.

I was so active in the sports department that I managed to organize "friendly matches" with the neighboring schools—which was a first for the area. These accomplishments were punctuated by my good performance in class, and the winning combination of successes earned me a great deal of influence and favor, not only among students but also among the teaching and non-teaching staffs. This was always a valuable asset which provided leverage in negotiating issues related to my financial obligations to the school. I created an air of indispensability, whereby the school could not afford to lose me. I became, for them, a highly valued asset. Suffice it to note that my actions were always deliberate.

At the end of the trimester, I took my academic report to St. Matia Mulumba and presented it to the secretary who played a significant role in finding part of my tuition. This time I found a bigger team of priests, sisters and directors, who looked as if they were conducting a meeting. Of course,

I was aware that I was not officially on the scholarship beneficiaries list. However, out of courtesy, I thought I owed it to the secretary to show her my report. I wanted to show her that the money was not going to waste, and I wished to explore prospects for the subsequent trimester. What I did not realize is that I was placing her in a rather precarious position.

While I hurried to place my report on the desk where reports of official beneficiaries are kept, she noticed me and intercepted. She immediately gave me an assignment to go to State House (the official president's office and residence) in Nakasero, an upscale place in Kampala city, and tell a gentleman named Paul Musoke that he was needed at our office immediately. I innocently left and headed straight for State House. I was a bit nervous, as it was my first time in such an environment. I presented my school identity card and went through all the tight security checks. The security detail asked me who I was looking for, as the name "Paul Musoke" didn't seem to register. I checked with all the departments and still couldn't find anyone by that name.

After a while, I had to return to the foundation, dejected and disappointed for failing to deliver on such a "minor" assignment. I was worried that the lady who had offered to bail me out of my desperate situation was not going to be amused by my failure. When I reached her office, I told her that there was no such person working in State House. All her colleagues had left. "Did you really go to State House?" she asked in shock. After pausing for a few moments, she broke into prolonged laughter. She couldn't believe that I had reached the president's office because she didn't think I even knew its location in the first place. She explained that the

Chess Strategy:

Be flexible. It seldom goes the way you planned. There will always be some surprise moves that require readjustment to continue.

Life Lesson:

Handle transitions wisely. Prepare for the unexpected. Learn to recompose and move again.

Nuggets of Wisdom:

1. Change is the only constant
2. Opposition can make us stronger
3. Don't give up; this too shall pass
4. It's not over until it is over

"Life is like riding a bicycle. To keep your balance, you must keep moving."

- Albert Einstein

"Greatness is often born in the cauldron of suffering and pain, where the abilities to maintain perspective and walk in forgiveness are learnt. It is in the hard places, the lonely places that we discover if we really have an all-consuming purpose or sense of destiny."

- Julia Cameron

reason she asked me to go to the State House was to deflect attention from the both of us, as it was probable her colleagues' interests would be piqued, and they would question how I was connected to their project.

I felt embarrassed for having made a fool of myself at State House searching for a non-existent person. Thinking back on it now, I realize it was also dangerous for me—I could have been arrested and charged for criminal trespass. I handed my report to the secretary, and as much as she appreciated it, she was quick to remind me that things were getting tight and that she could not guarantee any balances as was the case the previous trimester. I returned to Mukono after receiving this piece of discouraging news and picked up my routine chores at home.

I prayerfully went back to St. Matia Mulumba Foundation one week into the second trimester. The secretary had tried to accumulate some balances, but she told me that I needed to wait for another week to make it at least 100,000 shillings. Thankfully, when I returned at the appointed time, she had raised the amount, which I immediately deposited at school.

During the second trimester, the school scheduled elections for the student leadership. Even though I was approached by a couple of fellow students to run, I was ineligible according to the school regulations. Apparently, only students in the boarding section could assume leadership. However, to everybody's surprise (and mine), the headteacher told me to stand for the position of Sports Minister. I could not believe that the custodian of the school rules was the one bending them just because he wanted me to assume a position of leadership! I wound up competing, and, quite unsurprisingly, I was voted into the position of Games Minister (Student Sports Minister).

Following my attainment of the position, I was admitted into the boarding section of the school without being required to pay any additional tuition. When I shared the news with Auntie Dez, she could not believe what I was telling her. She thought I was merely joking or pulling a prank on her. But it was not fiction; it was the sweet truth.

I borrowed a bicycle from a friend to carry my belongings to school. They were not much: a small mattress, towel, blanket and bedsheets. I would undoubtedly be the only student at school who didn't own a suitcase. To start with, I had nothing to keep in there because once I reached school, I would set up my bed and all that I had to my name would be laid out before me. After loading my belongings on the bike, there was no space left to sit, so we ended up pushing

Chess Strategy: Challenge Yourself

If you only play equals, you never really improve. Take on a few tough challenges, and even if you lose, try to learn something new from the experience.

Life Lesson: Have Courage

Courage is your greatest ally. It is not until you exert a force greater than the weight of the object you wish to move that you will move it.

Nuggets of Wisdom:

When the going gets tough, the tough get going. Don't get pinned down. Where something more cherished cannot be brought into play because it is stuck behind something trivial, make every effort to get it into the game as soon as possible.

"Courage doesn't always roar. Sometimes courage is the little voice at the end of the day that says I'll try again tomorrow."

- Mary Anne Radmacher

"Sometimes even to live is an act of courage."

- Seneca

the bike all the way to school. Student leaders enjoyed some special privileges such as staying in our own private rooms, which we famously referred to as "state house."

Meanwhile, the school football team that I helped to start was registering steady progress. We competed favorably in several matches and even advanced to the national inter-school competitions level. We dominated football in our region as I continued to act as coach-cum-player. I had to work exceedingly hard to strike a balance between my academics, which were a priority to me, sports, and my ministerial responsibilities.

At the end of the term, I had performed very well in all my science subjects and excitedly took my report to the secretary at St. Matia Mulumba Foundation. Unfortunately, I was told that the lady had left the foundation. When I tried to prod further for her whereabouts—perhaps she could still help to maneuver on my behalf with the person that replaced her—I was informed that she had not only resigned her job, but also found new work and relocated to the UK. This news hit me like a brick to the face!

All books have an ending, and even plays have an anticlimax, but what kind of drama was mine that never had an end? Who or what would break this cycle of crisis once and for all? Life had totally denied me the prospect of ever settling in any comfort zone. It seemed to me that I was doomed to remain on tenterhooks, as I had never experienced a sustained period of happiness in my life.

I had to come to terms with the fact that my tuition honeymoon from the good secretary had finally come to an end. There was no way the new person would ever understand our "balance" arrangements as discussed only with the predecessor, so I didn't bother to even go there. Instead, I went straight to the headteacher and broke the news to him. I quickly thought of a solution to my problem. I proposed to the headteacher that he let me take on some casual labor during holidays. After all, I was good at maintaining gardens. My would-be payment could be converted into school fees. He was incredibly gracious and agreed to my proposal. His generosity could have been a way of returning the favor for the good things I was doing for the school, or for my good grades… but I'd like to think that maybe it was just his good nature.

Whatever the case, I was relieved that, once again, another door had opened where one had shut me out. The implication was that there were no more holidays for me while I was still studying. That meant that as other students were breaking off, I would have to hang around until the beginning of the following term. I guess my new title then was that of "student-servant" or "slave-student," however you would like to look at it. I informed the school matron about this development; about how I would be tending to the school compound, mowing the grass, keeping it clean and supporting the group renovating the school. The matron offered to provide me with some food during the holidays, a very welcome relief to me. Additionally, the head teacher assigned me more manual duties at his home. He also offered to provide a few things like sugar and other minor supplies.

During third term (Christmas) holidays, I went back home to Mukono. In order to raise money that would help me at school the next year, I went on a searching spree for petty jobs around the community. The kind of work I was looking for included manual labor at building sites and any related tasks. One day I was blessed to be hired by Mr. Sekatawa, one of the wealthy people in the locale, as part of a group that was to dig a fish pond. Sekatawa worked in the Office of the President and was a respected member of the community. I spent four straight weeks digging the large fish pond using hand tools, working tremendously hard every day with very few breaks. I was looking forward to a handsome pay for my hard work, hoping that I wouldn't have to struggle with personal needs the following term at school. Unfortunately for me, I did not receive a single coin for my hard labor.

The foreman hired by Mr. Sekatawa to supervise the work and pay the workers took me for a ride and disappeared into thin air when it came time to receive payment. I had no choice but to count it as a loss. I guess by now such things had lost their shock value to me. I understood the final year in my high school was going to be a do-or-die affair for me. I had no choice but to pull out all the stops and produce the kind of results that would help me secure a government scholarship at the university, available only for students who are able to meet a certain academic cutoff point. The government scholarship program is an extremely competitive program that takes only a few hundred students out of tens of thousands of candidates. Those who dominate the program usually come from the big or prestigious schools with the best teachers and facilities. I did not have any of those advantages to back me. I had only myself to depend on if I was to pull this off.

The good thing is that the worries of tuition were no more; I was now on a full bursary offered by the head teacher, or I should call it "working for my full tuition" following the arrangement I had with the school. That means I did not have to worry anymore about the financial aspect but instead focus all my efforts on the overarching goal of making it to the university. Most students thought that I was related to the head teacher with all the favors that I received from him. First, he allowed me to study with less than half the tuition at admission. Next, I had a waiver of school rules to let me stand for Games Minister, and now I was studying for free—which is very uncommon in a private school setting. Much to everyone's surprise, there was not even a sliver of relationship between us; even our names belong to different ethnicities. However, some students somehow found out that I used to stay at school during holidays to work. A group of students, especially those who wanted to taunt me, started referring to me as *SD*. I later learned that it meant *School Dependent*. I paid no attention to such insults; after all, I had set goals to achieve that required my focus every minute of my life.

Our school continued to excel in sports, particularly in football, where we won several trophies. My contribution in terms of sports was the only way I could pay back the school for granting me the opportunity to study for free and all the other attendant favors that came with it. However, some of my teachers were really concerned that I was investing way too much of my time in sports at the expense of my studies. They advised me to cut down on games and pay more attention to books, especially since the academic year was coming to an end. Most of them did not know that I was still in the school system in the first place because of sports. I could not even raise funds to pay for the mandatory exam registration. I had to approach a friend, Bestine Wemali from Kenya, to foot that bill, and she obliged. She wasn't doing so well in the Ugandan education system, and she always ran to me for help in almost all the subjects we studied. There was another debt that had accumulated on my school account accruing from other school requirements, but I requested the school to allow me to register so that I could work and pay all debts during my vacation after the exams.

Almost as if on cue, misfortune struck again during my third and final trimester at school. Once again, it was on the football pitch, bringing back the gruesome images in Lubiri S.S when I had a close brush with death. This time I was pushed by a teammate and hit the ground awkwardly, twisting my right hand around my wrist. This is the same hand that I use for writing, and the time for final exams was fast approaching in a matter of weeks. I was rushed to the hospital, and the doctor immediately recommended surgery because the X-ray report indicated that the wrist bones had gotten dislocated.

I was given an appointment for surgery, but after learning that the operation would make me miss my final exams, I intentionally skipped it and did not show up at Mulago Referral Hospital—which just so happened to be the same hospital where I was treated for my head injury. I instead went for a massage every morning and evening at a friend's house and spent time training my left hand to write as a potential substitute just in case the exams came before I recuperated. I thought training to use the left hand would be easy; after all, I just trained how to use the left leg. But this proved to be an uphill battle and an untenable task—a far cry from training my left foot to shoot goals. This was a whole different ball game.

There was only a month left before my final exams would begin, and my right hand was nowhere close to healing. Out of both concern and sympathy, the headteacher advised that I relax and give myself sufficient time to recover and skip the exams until the following year. Bad idea! The prospect of sitting for a full year because of a wrist dislocation, given the circumstances under which I made it thus far, did not sit well with me. I told him that since I had prepared well for the exams, I would rather give it a try and fail than fail to try. At this point, I was willing to accept any challenge that might come my way. I was ready to use my left hand and write like a kindergartener—anything other than missing the exam. Besides, there was half a chance that the pain would subside before D-day. Those who were familiar with my pain must have been wondering what kind of mettle I was made of. For me, this was more than sheer determination; it was my life. Only I knew what was truly at stake. Completing the exam was non-negotiable for me. Under different circumstances, I am sure I would have conveniently shelved the exam and basked in the abundance of sympathy for me. However, I did not have the luxury of sympathizers. I had no mother or father to run to, and the rest were already suffering from donor exhaustion. I had only myself to run to, and I could not let pain stand in my way!

Upon completion of my final high school exams, I returned to Auntie Dez's place. One year had already passed since I first went there. Unable to believe my story about joining boarding school, she had informed my other aunties that I had escaped from her home under the pretext of joining boarding school. She did not think I could be in school without any money for tuition or upkeep. During my stay at school, none of them had bothered to visit me to find out what was going on in my life. I could, therefore, forgive their disbelief and ignorance.

One of my friends who used to take me to play football for other teams as a mercenary had a car. At the end of my course, I contacted him with the request to bring me and my belongings back to Auntie Dez's house in Kiwanga, and he was kind enough to do so. I discovered that my colleague John Lukwago had left for the city, and he had gotten a job washing cars in Katwe at Kaguje Pub washing bay.

In preparation to join university, I needed to work and find resources to cater for requirements and my personal needs just in case I would make it to the university on government support for the top performers in the country. I teamed up with a group of men who were brickmakers, and they taught me their trade. At the same time, I landed another deal from Mr. Sekatawa, who owned a fish pond. He wanted it cleared of all the grass and the adjacent land leveled in preparation for the creation of a recreational ground with gardens. He contracted one of his relatives called Bosco, who hired me to work with him. The work was labor-intensive and had a tight deadline attached to it. Bosco had informed me that payment would be made upon completion, and I took him by his word since he was a relative to the boss. I worked hard till the very end when Mr. Sekatawa inspected the place and gave it a nod.

To my complete shock (perhaps I shouldn't have been), Bosco disappeared with my money. I frantically hunted for him for over two months trying to hold him accountable because all the while he was claiming that Sekatawa had not yet cleared him. When I got a chance to meet Mr. Sekatawa, he

Chess Strategy: Maximize Your Options

Keep your options open and take well calculated risks. Always have an escape route.

Life Lesson: Stay Positive

Face adversity head-on with a positive attitude. At times, the lessons attained from the experiences are better than the paycheck.

Nuggets of Wisdom:

The world is full of malicious people that will seek to pull food out of your mouth and push you off the cliff. Adversity should never define you; you have to fight a good fight and never give up.

"All too often, it is audacity and not talent that moves an artist to the center."

– Julia Cameron

"In any situation, the best thing you can do is the right thing; the next best thing you can do is the wrong thing; the worst thing you can do is nothing."

– Theodore Roosevelt

confirmed to me that he paid Bosco all the money in advance because he stated he needed to pay workers on a daily basis. I also learned that Bosco was his in-law—not a blood brother as Bosco used to claim. The next time I heard of Bosco, I heard that he had relocated from Kiwanga to another place in Kampala. It broke my heart that men had mastered the art of taking me for a ride, cheating me and using me left and right. This was now beginning to get on my nerves! Previously I worked in this same locale on Sekatawa's project for a whole two months and received practically nothing. Now it had happened again. I wondered who else was waiting to exploit me and hoped that I had learned my lesson from being taken advantage of so many times.

Following the disappointment with Sekatawa's pond project, I still needed to raise money to pay for my outstanding dues at school that had accumulated from school requirements. I decided to move to Auntie Mbakwanye's place in Katwe to link up with John Lukwago and get recruited in the car washing business. Being new at the station, I didn't have any customers, so I would instead be sub-contracted to wash the tires or clean carpets. My payment was usually about thirty cents whenever sub-contracted. However, my hands started developing painful blisters and deep cuts from cleaning mudguards using my bare hands, as the use of gloves was almost unheard of at the time. I washed cars every day for about two months while keeping my money with Aunt Mbakwanye. At that time, she was working as a cook for laborers at a construction site. It dawned on me that working on construction sites was better paying than washing cars as a so-called "sub-contractor." The least paid casual laborer there earned around 3,000 shillings a day (about $2 at that time).

I decided to work at the construction site where Aunt Mbakwanye cooked. I was lucky she was there before me because she introduced me to the Indians who were in charge of the project, which made it easy for me to get recruited immediately. We would work the whole day, carrying sand up the stairs of the multi-level building. At the end of the week, we would all be paid. I was working very hard with minimal resting time, if at all, because the Indians were using time rate. Consequently, the Indians were very strict on time and they would only grant us a one-hour lunch break.

I routinely handed over all my money to Auntie Mbakwanye to keep for me. It was during this time that our exam results were released. So, when I completed my week, I asked Auntie Mbakwanye to give me all the money I had saved with her so that I could go back to Kiwanga. She told me to proceed and that she would send the money to me. So, I went back to Auntie Dez's in Mukono and prepared to go to school and check on my results. Upon reaching the school campus, I was received like a hero. The teachers all came over to hug and congratulate me, thanking me for performing well. I had passed with high grades, although there was no guarantee that I would be considered for a government scholarship yet. Remember, I wrote my exams using a dislocated wrist. It had gotten better, but it still looked somewhat deformed.

Aunt Dez was excited as well, and she even confessed that she was not sure whether I had really sat for exams. I had happily surprised her. Meanwhile, I waited for Auntie Mbakwanye to send my money. As you may have guessed, history seemed to repeat itself yet again. She repeatedly told me stories until she finally confessed that she had used the money. Apologizing, she promised she would refund it soon. To date, that money has never seen the light of day. Luckily enough, my good performance on exams caused the school to waive the dues on my school account.

I waited with bated breath for the government selection lists to find out if I had been considered for a scholarship. Meanwhile, I was playing lots of football from which I continued to save some money. This time I kept it myself; remember, "Once bitten, twice shy." Whenever I raised a substantial amount, I would purchase an item and keep it with Auntie Dez. I bought a blanket, towel, bedcover and other items in preparation for life at the university.

From all the time I spent with my different aunties, I learned to do every conceivable kind of work. I learned to do house chores and to tend to the garden. I dug pit latrines, and even graves! The injustices and countless forms of exploitation that I was subjected to by so many people instilled in me a high degree of tolerance and prepared me for the unexpected.

I had worked very hard in my senior high with hopes that I could qualify for the civil engineering degree on government scholarship. As well as I had performed, there was no guarantee that I would fit within the cutoff points for the course I wanted. After the time of selection, the lists of the students to be sponsored by the government were released. Remembering the courses we applied for, we each stormed the respective faculties to check for our placements. Walking up to my first pick, I didn't find my name at the civil engineering department at Makerere University. I felt a surge of adrenaline cause my heart to race, and fear threatened to consume me. I started shaking and wondered what I had to do next. I spent a whole day at the campus, carefully checking each list name by name from the faculties I had applied for... but this time my search was in vain.

Frustrated and weary, I walked back to Mukono that night. I couldn't bear to eat any food, feeling let down and discouraged. In the morning, I walked to my former school to talk to Mr. Mugisha, the registrar. Upon reaching the school, I received warm welcomes and celebrations that I had gotten a place on government. Equally flattered and confused, I asked them what university I had gotten placed. The teacher told me I had been placed at Makerere University! I was shocked. Knowing that I had checked on every list I expected my name to appear, I asked him to elaborate on what had transpired. The registrar informed me that I had been given a placement for the Bachelor of Science degree in the faculty of Science Education. It finally dawned on me that I hadn't checked those lists. The registrar added that it was a flat degree in sciences, where most people end up teaching in the respective subjects they are given.

I went back to Makerere to confirm what I had just heard. They were able to verify that, yes, my name was on the list of those to pursue the Bachelor of Science in Physics and Math. After gathering more info about the course, I learned that those who take it don't specialize in anything particular and that is the reason it is regarded as a flat course. I didn't like what I heard. I needed to specialize in something if I expected to increase my chances for a better life.

Eventually, I learned that there was a possibility of requesting a change of course. I collected more info on how that was done, and I was told I needed to have someone of influence to help me pursue the change of course. I wondered to myself who my person of influence could possibly be. I went back to Mukono pondering this question, attempting to figure out what I needed to do. Having scanned through all my connections, I decided to approach the registrar Mr. Mugisha to see if he would be willing to pursue this change for me. The change required me to go to the selection center with all the documents, submit the change request and talk to the people in charge.

Surprisingly, there was no hesitation from the registrar. After discussing the possibilities for the change of course, he helped me put together the needed paperwork to present to the Joint Admission Board (JAB) that was responsible for the selections and placements. The decision we had come up with was to change from a degree to a diploma. So, my wish was that I would be granted the chance to switch from a flat degree to a diploma in Civil Engineering. It took us almost three weeks, but eventually the request was granted. However, it was not from Makerere; I was instead posted to Kyambogo University.

I pursued my engineering diploma and did well at all my internships, but after graduation, I had no chance for a job because I didn't know anyone in the top establishments, and for some opportunities, I was considered too qualified for the placements. I had to revert to teaching soccer in the slums as I waited for a job opportunity to pop up, and after a while, I introduced chess and started teaching it to the children. It felt like my engineering education had gone to waste.

However, in the course of social development work, I was the best candidate to lead construction projects in sports outreach. I have since used the same acquired skills to build Phiona's family house, Stellah Babirye's family house, and Lydia Nanona's family house. These are some of the children nurtured from the Chess Academy raised by single mothers. Many other people still come to me for guidance and advice in the same field. In other words, my diligence in pursuing a professional course wasn't in vain. In fact, it has been very instrumental in the construction developments of the Chess Academy, as well as my own house.

*"Nothing in life is to be feared,
it is only to be understood. Now
is the time to understand more,
so that we may fear less."*

– Marie Curie

CHAPTER FIVE
CHOOSE TO BE A BLESSING

I AM WHO I am today because a few incredible people took interest in me at different stages of my growth. They spotted the potential in me and acted as midwives—pushing my dreams into reality. The first of these people was Aloysius Kyazze. Aloysius was an accomplished football player with an impressive CV spanning over three decades. At the top of his career, he featured in the national team, the Uganda Cranes, as skipper and made a few rounds in Uganda's top league academies, including SC Villa and Express FC, among others. He even helped to start new football academies like Miracle FC and TOP Radio FC, which entered into the top-flight league within the second year of their formation—a significant feat by any standard. In addition to this, Aloysius was a man on a mission. He was a devout Christian who sought to use his gift in sports to touch the lives of the unchurched. He started Sports Outreach Ambassadors (SOA) football team, which was based in Lubiri Secondary School, where I spent my first years of secondary school/O'Level. His wife, Esther, was also very involved in SOA activities and was like a mother figure to the group.

Around 2001, SOA had a football match against Pepsi Cola FC on the Kyambogo University sports grounds. I was a student at that university by that time, although I was already playing academy football for Pepsi. The SOA team must have been impressed by my skillful display on the pitch that day, because they immediately asked me to join their team. I decided to take their invitation and joined SOA. Though Aloysius—and the majority of the team—were born-again Christians, they did not try to cajole me into becoming one. Instead, they implemented a systematic process of discipleship that eventually left members with little choice but to embrace what they believed. In 2003, Aloysius was recruited by Sports Outreach Ministry (SOM). He was invited by Russ Carr, the founder and head of the Sports Outreach Institute, based in the U.S. I was also asked to join Sports Outreach as an instructor.

*

At this point in the story, it's important to note that without me having met Aloysius and having joined SOA, you might not be reading this book. Without Aloysius, I would never have joined Sports Outreach, I might not have been able to reconnect to the slums, and I wouldn't have founded the SOM Chess Academy and the Robert Katende Initiative. I would not have been able to create and establish programs that reach out to vulnerable children, including disabled kids, to restore hope and transform lives through chess, one move at a time. Instead, I would probably be working on construction sites somewhere in line with my civil engineering skills. I have no idea what kind of life I would be leading now if it weren't for Aloysius. He sowed a seed in me at a critical time: a desire to lift others up from the pits to a place of meaning. My wife's involvement in SOM is very reminiscent of the active engagement of Aloysius' wife, Esther, in Sports Outreach. They paved the way for others to follow in their footsteps, and we are incredibly grateful.

Given my history of enduring suffering of many kinds, I have developed a strong sense of respect for all people, regardless of their prevailing circumstances or creed. When I look back at where I came from—the sense of hopelessness that I struggled with for years, how people picked me up here and there and helped me to climb the pedestal of hope—I feel it is my duty to do the same for others. I have vowed to never look down upon anyone, regardless of their upbringing or differences. I have

Chess Strategy: Sacrifice

Be prepared to sacrifice material for position. Sometimes even the greatest material sacrifice can result in a winning position later on.

Life Lesson: Negativity Captivity

Seize each opportunity.

There are many opportunities that we encounter daily. Sometimes we recognize them, but oftentimes we don't. Don't be so fixated on the negatives that you miss the good opportunities that come your way through trials. You must, by all means, avoid the captivity of negativity.

Nuggets of Wisdom

1. See challenges as opportunities
2. Learn to leverage each opportunity
3. Weigh options and build a strategy

"The true nature of the heart is seen in the face of the unattractive."

– ANONYMOUS

learned from experience that God can raise anyone from the dust and lead them to dine with royalty. If we look around, there are endless examples of people who have left a mark on this world; people who were once nobodies but managed to rise high above their circumstances and become influencers of society.

Having this in mind, I always treat everyone with respect, no matter their social status, appearance, or position. You never know, the acquaintance you take for granted because he or she is going through unpleasant circumstances—which I refer to as training—could turn out to assume a position of power that results in you bowing down before him, as was the case with the story of Joseph in the Bible. There is a proclivity of the human heart to be attracted to the good and resist the unappealing. We tend to only associate with people who fit our class, network with those of the same educational achievements, hang out in places that reflect our status and so on. Some people call it keeping up appearances. Our hearts are constantly put to the test whenever we have to deal with people we deem to be below our station. We are not mindful of the fact that life is like a series of ladders—some are climbing, while others are descending.

I am witnessing, on a regular basis, young people who have emerged from the miry swamps of Katwe and other underserved communities turn around to scale professional heights and become resourceful citizens. These castaways are now starting their own private clinics, teaching in prestigious institutions, and traversing the world thanks to their mastery of the game of chess. *The Queen of Katwe* will forever remain an indelible imprint on the memory of the world.

This amazing true story stands as a classic example of how a pawn can make its way through all manner of opposition and assume the status of a queen. Phiona Mutesi, the principle subject of the book and reenacted character in the movie is, by all means, a work in progress. Hers is a heart-rending, tear-jerking account that has won acclaim all over the world. It was so gruesome that many people who read the book and saw the movie had to ask whether it was really true. My answer to them remains the same: What they see in the film is nowhere near the actual severity of the harsh reality it attempts to depict.

What Phiona and her family, as well as the other families in the movie, went through is far more debilitating than words or pictures on the screen can convey.

Phiona is now pursuing a Bachelor of Science as a business major at Northwest University in Kirkland, Washington. She is still excelling in chess, winning medals for her university as well as her country. Her life will never be the same again. She is clearly destined to live out the role of "The Queen of Katwe" in real life. The world is keenly watching her every move, both on the chessboard and in her daily life, waiting to place the real crown on her head.

*

In order to flourish in the kind of work that I do now, I needed to experience hardship and endure suffering to be able to connect with people well. My story resonates with many people in many situations that I encounter on a daily basis. Since I have lived in a ghetto before, I understand the ghetto language and social infrastructure. I can relate to slum

Chess Strategy

Mastering chess requires hard work: facing tough opponents and enduring defeats to learn from them.

Life Lesson: Positivity

Think positive. What doesn't break you makes you.

Nuggets of Wisdom

1. See yourself as victorious
2. Make a new path where none exists; don't be afraid to try
3. Be success-driven

"Difficulties and adversities viciously force all their might on us and cause us to fall apart, but they are necessary elements for individual growth and to reveal our true potential. We have got to endure and overcome them and move forward. Never lose hope. Storms make people stronger and never last forever."

– Roy T. Bennett

dwellers with utmost ease. I have been abandoned by my parents and left with nothing, so I can relate to orphans and those whose parents have abdicated their duties and responsibilities. On the other hand, I also had people who sincerely believed in me and offered me a chance to rehabilitate and realize my potential. Now I am doing just that: picking up and restoring the rejects and giving them an opportunity to thrive and rise to the top.

Still, I cannot claim to be perfect. I believe I am very much a work in progress, just like the many people around me for whom I am responsible. But the one thing I am sure of is that the pain I've endured and the struggles I've faced have not been for nothing. I can now identify with the Apostle Paul's declaration in Philippians 4:11-13, "Now that I speak in respect of want: for I have learned, in whatsoever state I am, to be content. I know both how to be abased, and I know how to abound: everywhere and in all things, I am instructed both to be full and to be hungry, both to abound and to suffer need. I can do all things through Christ who strengthens me." (KJV)

It is never easy to embrace hardship and pain, but as you walk through life, you may find it inevitable. Throughout my childhood, I don't remember experiencing much happiness. I could probably count the number of times I smiled on one hand, and they were mostly on the football pitch. Even when happy moments came, within a short while something worse was lurking in the shadows, waiting to pounce and inflict more misery. However, these countless hostile circumstances helped me learn to cope with every situation. I trained my mind to be prepared for the unexpected, and it enabled me to adapt to any environment.

Being a mentor to hundreds of children faced with a multiplicity and diversity of challenges turned out to be a full-time job for me the instant I ventured out into the Sports Outreach Ministry—more than a decade and a half ago. It has been both joyful and stressful; a draining yet rewarding adventure that dictates every single day of my life. I am inevitably sucked into the personal issues of the children and their families, called to intervene in very intimate matters. Many of these families lack father figures, and because of my close relationship with them, I inadvertently take on the role of head of household by default. In turn, I have the responsibility of taking the lead on advising in all crucial decisions. It is quite emotionally demanding to be a part of the excruciating and traumatic experiences of countless families and still maintain a positive outlook on life. The one thing that has kept my spirit alive and my head high has been an enduring hope—always planning for the worst and hoping for the best. Born in poverty without any assurance of education, I am constantly reminded that I was blessed to have people invest in me while growing up, and thus, it behooves me to be a blessing to others.

To be a blessing is not limited to a pattern of material giving. In most cases, it only requires one to stand with those in need and offer encouragement and support and help them learn to make better decisions through the challenging circumstances they face. In today's society, we have somehow bought into the lie that all people need money to turn around their situations. However, some of these men and women ended up in these situations for reasons that have nothing to do with money or material things. In this case, giving them money with the hope that it will fix them is like throwing seeds in the bush and hoping that somehow, they will sprout and yield bountifully.

Sometimes, investing our time, knowledge and wisdom in others is far more precious than any material contribution. You cannot give away what you don't have. All I had was my leadership ability. Teaching people to manage their time while keeping their goals in mind, whether short or long-term, is invaluable. "Give a man a fish, and you feed him for a day. Teach a man to fish, and you feed him for a lifetime." (author unknown) From this proverb alone, we can see that what is most effective in helping someone to turn their lives around is taking the time to teach them how to use what they already possess within themselves.

Be mindful not to coddle, but rather to mentor; this means that in addition to your support and encouragement, they also benefit from rebuke when necessary.

My first years of deep involvement in the lives of the children in the Katwe ghetto was with the pioneers of the SOM Chess Academy: the Academy was an entity I founded in 2004 with a single chessboard. We started out with a larger group playing football, and later I introduced them to the game of chess. Besides the beauty of chess being a metaphor for life, it was more inclusive and convenient in regard to the infrastructure of the slums. The large number of children who were first interested in chess soon dwindled to a handful, and we finally settled at a group of six youngsters who chose to hang in for a while and became permanent additions to the program. Beyond the chess game and the free porridge meal, I became interested in their lives. At that time, I didn't have the resources to make any meaningful personal interventions beyond the cup of porridge we shared and the life discussions and lessons we had. The local leadership of Sports Outreach never embraced the program, and one time I was even accused of using football time for chess. I resorted to conducting chess sessions after the football training and would often leave the slums late in the evening around 8:00 p.m.

After almost a year of my running the chess program, Russ Carr, the president of Sports Outreach in the USA at the time, visited Uganda. I was completely unaware of the fact that he had been reading and following my monthly update letters. I used to share what I was doing in my personal time in each letter, and one of the things I mentioned was teaching chess to the slum kids. To the surprise of the local leadership of Sports Outreach, he had brought a few plastic chessboards with him to support the chess program. Of course, the chessboards were sorely needed, but to me, the recognition of the chess program by the president was far more important. After coming to visit, he began giving monthly contributions of $50 towards the program. This support changed the perspective of the top leaders of Sports Outreach at that time, and they started recognizing the chess program as an important part of ministry activities.

To me, it was a huge relief—this meant that the kids had an assurance of their cup of porridge throughout the month. In 2006, three of the kids from the chess program were considered for a tuition scholarship by Sports Outreach. Seeing the children have an opportunity to attend school was a breakthrough for me, and in order to encourage this support, it prompted me to call the program *SOM Chess Academy*. The kids shared similar challenges of broken families, poverty and low self-esteem. One of the things I sought to instill in them was a sense of leadership, which was severely lacking among the adult fraternity in the slum. I saw the potential to start afresh with these youngsters as the beacon of hope for the broken community that was Katwe.

In 2003, during the very first year of the SOM Chess Academy in Katwe, I identified 10-year-old Richard Tugume as a potential leader. Richard was staying with his aunt and dad in a 10-by-10-foot room in the sprawling Katwe ghetto. He joined SOM and played football for a year before abandoning it to be part of the Chess Academy. He was among the six kids who formed the first permanent group. After spending one year out of school due to lack of tuition, I recommended him for the SOM education fund, through which he was able to join Primary 5 in 2006. I charged him with the responsibility of keeping the only chessboard that we possessed at the time. It was a standard chess set that I had framed in a glass seal for protection and durability. Richard did a great job keeping the board, and he was always on time bringing it in for the chess sessions.

One evening, he took me aside and whispered to me, "Coach, we need to find somewhere else to keep our chessboard." A look of deep concern spread across his face, and I knew something was wrong.

"Why would you want to give up the duty when you're doing a great job keeping the board?"

"It has nothing to do with me wanting to give it up," he replied. "Last night it nearly got broken!"

"Broken?" I was not expecting to hear that. "How? What happened?"

"My dad. He returned home very drunk, as usual, and had a fierce fight with my aunt in the room. It is only by miracle that our chessboard survived!" he said, relieved. He added that he was not ready to risk putting the board in harm's way because of the recklessness of his father; he would rather find another place to keep it.

The first chessboard was a treasured possession for us at that time. It was one of the few assets that brought us together as a family. Its destruction would spell real doom for us because a replacement was not guaranteed. Richard Tugume seemed to appreciate the value of the board so much that he was more concerned about its safety than that of himself and his aunt, who had to endure days and nights of torment from his inconsiderate and irresponsible father. I could see that it took a sense of responsibility for Richard to figure this out, which is a crucial ingredient of leadership.

I understood and appreciated Richard's sincere concern for the safety of our chessboard. But deep inside, I was more troubled by the domestic violence that he and several other kids were experiencing. The situation prompted me to strategize on how I could confront the conflict in an amiable manner that would not endanger the boy's life. I began by accompanying him back home and met his aunt. His father was rarely at home during the day. It took me a couple of months of walking Richard home before I finally met him. It just so happened to be right after I had secured a scholarship opportunity for Richard's education. I needed his father to provide some details for the paperwork, so I had a strong reason to hunt him down. Luckily enough, I was getting closer to the aunt, so it worked in my favor as she would also speak on my behalf. Eventually, I built a strong bond with the entire family that yielded some serious talks with them, particularly concerning young Tugume. Soon after the confrontation, the violence in their house became a thing of the past.

Even after experiencing the hopelessness that comes with violence, Tugume worked his way up both the education ladder and the chess game with unprecedented passion. After finishing primary school at Molly and Paul School, he joined St. Mbuga Vocational Secondary School—still on the SOM scholarship. He immediately became part of the school chess club, which he captained between 2012 and 2014, playing board one all the while. He went on to win the 2011 Rwabushenyi National Chess Championship for the unrated category and has also won the annual SOM Interproject Tournament three times. As of the writing of this book, he has completed his Bachelor of Information Technology and Computing degree at Kyambogo University in Kampala in 2018. He was part of the university chess team, where he has won several accolades. In 2015 and 2016, he took part in the East African Inter-University Games at Jomo Kenyatta University in Kenya, playing board one, in which they won gold for the team. In the 2017 edition of the same Inter-University games, he again played board one and won gold. He currently works as an administrator and instructor at the SOM Chess Academy in Katwe.

Richard Tugume is not alone in this type of story; he is just one of many amazing examples of kids that have waded through the mire of the Katwe ghetto to reclaim a place on the national chess high table. Discovering some of these kids required that I bend regulations, but it usually turned out I had an uncanny ability to spot talent.

In 2008, my eyes were on Joan Nakimuli, one of the young girls at the Chess Academy who used to bring her siblings to the program. I knew they were staying with a single mother who couldn't afford to pay her rent. Eventually, I decided to intervene and contribute to help them pay their rent for a single dingy room. It was situated in one of the worst possible places within the slum, at the spot where murky water from all directions converged into a small lake that would extend into their room with even the smallest amount of rain. They had stuffed a bed and worn sofa in the tiny space, leaving hardly any room to walk. The family of five would somehow squeeze in the room every night. On a bad rainy day, they would have to sit up on the bed and chair as the water would reach knee-deep, soaking every single possession they had. It would take nearly three days for the water to subside, also resulting in three days of no sleep. It was pointless to scoop out the water because the water levels outside were the same as those in the house! They endured this situation for years on end. But that was not all. They also had to go days without a morsel of food to eat. At some point, their mother, Gertrude Nanono, gave up the fight and had determined to commit suicide rather than see her children perish before her own eyes.

One day, Joan shared with me that they had spent three nights without eating dinner. The meal they had at the Chess Academy would see them through the 24 hours until the next day's meal at the Academy. The bigger problem was that their mother had gone missing without leaving behind any notice. In my eyes, I had no choice but to help them out. First, I had to deal with the issue of food. Despite having just enough in reserve to carry the Academy program through the week, I decided to give them some beans and corn flour for their dinner. I then took it upon myself to mount a search for the missing mother, starting in the immediate neighborhood. I could not find any useful leads. No one seemed to have a clue where she could have gone. And I don't blame them—how could they possibly know when every family was fighting their own battles? In any case, I was incredibly concerned about this situation. I asked the neighbors to keep watch over the kids as I involved the local authorities. Fortunately, the following day, the children told me when they came for the chess program that their mother had returned that very night and that she was ecstatic when she found food at home. She asked the children to pass her gratitude to me. I was tremendously relieved with this news.

The following day, I went with the kids to their home after our program to find out what had caused her to do such a thing. Immediately after seeing me, she knelt down in full view of the neighbors and thanked me profusely for the food, which made me feel quite mortified. I asked to speak to her in private, and what she told me then left me in a complete state of shock. She said she had run away from the children because she didn't want to see them starve to death on her watch. She also shared that she had five children from three different men. She didn't know the whereabouts of two of the men and one had denied responsibility, claiming the child wasn't his. This left all the children fatherless.

She had no education at all, and the petty trade she tried to engage in at the market was yielding nothing. Life was utterly hopeless, and everything had gone awry. She also added that she had disappeared to try and search for work, but she came back empty-handed. Her last resort was to kill both herself and her children on the night of her return by using the poison she had carried with her. Her plot was eerily reminiscent of my own situation years back when desperation drove me to the wall, and I opted for suicide by rat poison. It was all so weirdly parallel to my past; the only difference is that I could not afford the poison and she could. She confessed that if she hadn't come home to the donated food that night, we wouldn't be having this conversation. I requested that she hand me the poison immediately. Lo and behold, it was rat poison! I threw it in the pit latrine and began to thank God for the decision I had taken to provide the children some food just in the nick of time. It truly was a miracle.

This incident drew me even closer to Gertrude's family, and from that day on I began to visit them frequently—at least once a week. I encouraged her not to give up on life and to keep her hope alive; things would not stay the same way forever. I was moved to secure scholarships for three of her children in the Chess Academy, which provided an opportunity for them to go to school through support from Sports Outreach Ministry. This was a major breakthrough for her knowing that she would never have dreamed of her kids having an education when simply having a meal a day would be a miracle.

She continued to struggle with the rent of under $6 a month until 2010, when John Carls met one of the children during his first visit to Uganda. He had come as part of an advance team on behalf of Disney Studios for *The Queen of Katwe* movie project. When he got wind of Gertrude's situation, he was so moved with compassion that he decided to do something about it. He pledged to contribute towards their rent on a regular basis. Slowly, the veil of hell began to lift off Gertrude's family, as things were finally changing in her favor.

In 2012, when I started renting a house for the Chess Academy, I made the decision to move Gertrude's entire family into the Academy house. Due to the nature of property that they owned, ravaged by years of decay from murky flood water and bedbugs all over, I decided that they would not be bringing anything from the old shack. But that meant I had to purchase everything from mattresses to bedding. For the kids, it was their very first time sleeping on their own mattresses without fear of floods invading the house. This marked a major turning point for Gertrude and her family, and it meant the world to them. In return, Gertrude started helping out with the preparation of food for the children at the Chess Academy.

The tide of fortune seemed to continue favoring Gertrude's family in many ways. I managed to get Stella

Chess Strategy: Look for the Lifeline

We all blunder from time to time. This does not mean we should give up and run away. Often when you're sure there is no way out after a terrible mistake, you will be given a lifeline.

Life Lesson: Positive Outcomes Through Adversity

Channel adversity to create positive outcomes. Tolerance is a skill attained through experiences.

Nuggets of Wisdom

1. Avoid negative thinking; find "the rainbow in each cloud"
2. Become self-competitive
3. Develop the courage to face challenges
4. Adversity can build character or fuel despair—the choice is yours

"It is not enough that we do our best; sometimes we must do what is required."

– Winston S. Churchill

"Faith is not the belief that God will do what you want. It is the belief that God will do what is right."

– Max Lucado

Chess Strategy: Play Wisely

Each stage of the game is very important: opening, middle or end. How you start a game determines how you will progress and finish it. Play wisely.

Life Lesson: Passion, Hope and Faith

Develop a passion for the Game of life. Cling onto hope and take each move by faith.

Nuggets of Wisdom

1. The benefit of study and practice
2. Join chess clubs
3. Play online and in neighborhood chess matches

"A blind man's world is bounded by the limits of his touch; an ignorant man's world by the limits of his knowledge; a great man's world by the limits of his vision."

– E. Paul Hovey

"To bake a cake you must use flour, salt, raw eggs, sugar, and oil. Eaten individually, each is pretty distasteful or even bitter. But bake them together and they become delicious."

– ANONYMOUS

Babirye, one of her children, to audition for *The Queen of Katwe,* for which she was selected. Part of the proceeds from her acting remuneration went towards the acquisition of a plot of land several miles away from the Katwe slums in the countryside. They began to grow their own food on the land, which they would visit on weekends and during holidays. At the end of 2017, we mobilized resources and built them a family house on the property. They were able to move in just before Christmas—the greatest Christmas gift of their lives! This move into a place they would call their permanent home solidified the completion of their turnaround from the brink of a family suicide instigated by their mother to a happy family full of hope. All three children are doing their studies in secondary school and continue to excel in chess, winning lots of medals and trophies.

Who Needs to Be Blessed?

The story of the family of Gertrude Nanono is a real-life demonstration of what happens when all hope has vanished. Many people lose all meaning for life when the tide turns against them, and in turn, many choose to end their lives. This situation is not limited to the victims of the Katwe ghetto; it happens all over the world. As a matter of fact, statistics show that suicide is more prevalent in developed countries than it is in developing countries where life is seemingly worse.

As we touched on earlier, material wealth does not necessarily guarantee a blissful life. In fact, many people in developed countries where life is ostensibly easier profess the opposite. The South African author Francois Du Toit writes, "Many affluent people today are totally dependent on anti-depressants. Wealth and fame certainly do not guarantee a fulfilled life. Instead, depression has become the modern illness. Yet, in a sense, we have never had it any better. Science has given us remarkable medical breakthroughs to enable us to live longer and safer than ever before. There are more people alive today than the total number of people who ever died in the history of mankind." (Du Toit, 2005).

The entertainment of the senses has become the biggest industry of our times; think big-money sports, film, music, or travel, or the drug and porn industries. If ultimate fulfillment could be attained through entertainment, we should be the happiest people on the planet. We bombard our senses with high definition information and sensation; available at our fingertips in seconds. We have never traveled faster. Our children astound us with their technological skills, and we have so much available to us at the mere touch of a button, yet greed and a constant sense of lack seem to dominate both the rich and poor.

A BBC radio program a few years ago looked at levels of happiness of people in Britain over the last half-century. The program showed that the Britain of fifty years ago did not have the kind of social and cultural amenities—such as electric trains and recreation centers–that it boasts of now, reflecting the monumental transformations in society that have transpired since then. And yet, according to the radio show, research indicates that the British today are far less happy than those who lived half a century ago. The suicide rates have also multiplied exponentially since that time. This is a mystery that further debunks the idea that innovation and affluence can guarantee a better life and insulate mankind from the woes of purposeless living. The program noted that one of the happiest groups in the world are the Nigerians who live in a poor country in West Africa. All this serves to show that when it comes to certain elements of life, economic and social status may be of limited or no consequence.

I am constantly reminded by the stated hypothesis that the quest for the highest performance, as defined by the world, should not be our predominant objective. It is far more important to celebrate the small blessings that come our way daily. We are fortunate to be alive at all, and the fact that there is life means that there is hope. This is the reason I never give up on anyone, however hopeless the situation may seem. God can use and raise up anyone, and He loves to use people to accomplish His will. Choosing to be a blessing to others is one of the ways of recognizing this fact and acting on it.

I was able to get nine children from the Chess Academy into *The Queen of Katwe* movie auditions. This wasn't an easy feat, given that I had to take a fair amount of time to get them ready for the audition process. This audition would be competitive; they would not favor the kids just because they were from the Chess Academy or because some of the roles were a reenactment of their personal lives. Preparation involved teaching them how to conduct themselves in a formal setting, especially during the interviews. It was not easy to reorient them from the ghetto mentality that had permeated every aspect of their lives. Acting on a Disney set was almost tantamount to entering a new civilization from an ancient order. Of the nine candidates who auditioned, only four managed to make it through to the final cast. This still was a major achievement considering the kind of candidates they were pitted against!

But that seemed to be just the beginning of the battle; the process of getting the required paperwork and documents would turn out to be quite the challenge as well. For starters, not a single one of the four kids knew their date of birth, nor did their parents or guardians! To make matters more complicated, some of them had single mother households, and the mothers didn't know where the fathers were in order to obtain the necessary information. This turned out to be just like another cat and mouse chase, ironically resembling a chess game. Since I was directly responsible for the four kids, I had to be very creative in ensuring that they didn't miss out on the opportunity in front of them just because of personal information. I was required to process court affidavits to ensure that all bases were covered. I also had to process birth certificates for them, and this information could only be obtained from their relatives—that is, if they happened to have an idea of their year of birth. The month and date had to be guessed, and in some cases, the year had to be guessed as well. I asked the children their preferred dates and months of birth so they could memorize them, just in case they were asked to state their date of birth during the interviews.

Since Gloria Nansubuga's mother had disappeared a long time ago, as a way of improvising, I made Stella's mother act as her "mother" as well. Although she was illiterate, she agreed to stand in as the mother for both of them. Of course, they had to be from different fathers, because they had surnames from different clans. This wasn't an issue for her, as she already had six children with four different fathers. She played this role so well that I was even able to process passports for them.

For David Mubiru, who was 14 years old at the time, we had to search for his father. At least in his case, his mother had a clue where we could start. I reached out to one of the relatives and introduced myself, then traveled to the district where the father was staying. It definitely wasn't easy. At first, he thought that he was wanted for abandoning the children. But we eventually convinced him that I was not a government agent seeking to arrest him, rather I was on a mission to seek his help to benefit his own son. This turned out to be a great achievement—through this process, the children got a chance to reconnect with their father, even though he had nothing of material benefit to offer them. He was pleasantly surprised that I was processing a passport for his son to travel to South Africa.

In most cases, being the mentor for a child requires you to connect with the child's family, particularly if you want to see significant transformation. In most cases, it is the women who are available for the children either as single mothers, grandmothers or aunties. Having been personally brought up by a grandmother and aunties, I understood this well. I specifically remember a time I was having a conversation with a single mother who had two children in the Chess Academy. I encouraged her not to neglect her children and explained to her how her presence had a vital role in all of their lives. She grumbled about how each of her children had a different father, and that the men had abandoned their children and dumped her. She told me that she was simply "helping" the children because she technically could run away at any time. Her ancestral home was open and available for her to go and stay, away from the trouble of the so-called absentee fathers.

I couldn't believe what I was hearing. I challenged her to stay focused on her family and admonished her never to let circumstances cause her to deny her own, much like the men who had denied responsibility for their family. She had been toying with the idea of dragging those men to authorities for DNA testing to compel them to take responsibility. I talked her out of this idea for many reasons, one being the cost—she simply did not have the resources to pursue testing. This was one of those cases where I would find myself taking responsibility not only for children, but also for the adults.

In Uganda, mothers abandoning their children is quite a common phenomenon. Gloria and Benjamin had a mother who was staying with them after separating from her husband. Their life was a huge struggle, and she was overwhelmed with single-handedly carrying the burden. Her children joined the chess program at the Academy where they were immediately guaranteed a free meal once a day before being enrolled into the education program later. Even with these developments, she continued to face hardships and the time came when she could not keep up with the rent. She was forced to move in with her younger sister within the same neighborhood. In 2009, she told her sister that she was moving to Juba, South Sudan to try her luck with work there. I learned of this from her sister, nearly a month after her departure.

The sister continued struggling to care for the children by herself, until she finally got overwhelmed and started drowning under the weight of responsibility. It started with her defaulting on the rent, until she was eventually evicted from her room. Since she didn't want the children to miss out on school or lose the scholarship opportunity at the Chess Academy, her only option was to find another room in the ghetto. Having failed to find a space for rent, she decided to put up a makeshift timber structure above a drainage channel where she could stay with the children. This put her life and the lives of the children in great danger because the drainage channel was prone to flooding whenever it rained. The floodwater could easily sweep them away down the gutter if they dared stay there any more than a few days.

I discussed the situation with my wife Sarah, and we decided to take the two children, Gloria and Benjamin, into our care in the two-room house we occupied at that time. This was in addition to Phiona Mutesi, who was already staying with us. As of this writing, Benjamin is a second-year student at Northwest University in Kirkland, Washington, USA. It has now been nine years since their mother left them, and we have neither heard from her nor heard any rumors of her whereabouts. With the civil war that raged in South Sudan in 2010 claiming many lives, including Ugandans who worked there, we fear that she could have been among the innocent victims. There is no other logical answer that we can come up with, apart from the thought that maybe she could be somewhere in hibernation. We may never know for sure, but we will continue to keep our hope alive.

With Gloria and Benjamin staying in our home, we were able to monitor them closely. We noticed a steady improvement both in their discipline and their mastery of the game of chess. Benjamin Mukumbya was able to represent Uganda in Sudan in 2009, as well as Angola in 2014 for the Africa Junior Chess Championship. He later went on to compete in Abu Dhabi for the World Juniors. So far, Gloria Nansubuga has represented Uganda at the World Youth Chess Championships in South Africa in 2013, Greece in 2015 and, in 2018, she made it to the top Uganda Women's National team. She represented Uganda in the World Olympiad in Batumi, Georgia, along with Phiona and three other ladies: Ivy Amoko, Christine Namaganda and Penina Nakabo.

Gloria was one of the four children chosen from auditions to be part of *The Queen of Katwe* movie, which gave her an opportunity to travel to South Africa once again—this time as part of the cast in May of 2015. Thanks to her movie acting remuneration, she currently owns a plot of land in the countryside registered in her name, away from the slums. I managed to secure a plot of land for each of the four children from the Chess Academy who took part in the movie. Their mothers are incredibly thankful, as they travel to work on their plots where they currently grow their own food.

As mentioned earlier, Gertrude and her family had already built and moved into their house—something they had never imagined could happen in their lifetime. Lydia Nakato's family also now owns a house of their own. In June 2018, four students who went on a trip with Sports Outreach visited Lydia's family in Katwe. They were greatly moved by the living condition of Lydia, her mother and the four siblings of hers. They committed to raising some support so that they could build a house on their purchased plot of land. When they went back to the US, they shared with their church, and a family decided to be a blessing to Lydia's family. They donated $5,000, which I used to build them a house, using my engineering skills to circumvent some of the expenses. The plan is for all of them to eventually be able to put up a house for themselves and move in. Gloria is now in secondary school in Kampala. She hopes to complete high school in 2020.

These happy moments notwithstanding, there still remain challenges that must be addressed. For instance, the children occasionally suffer ill health, which requires seeing the doctor. It is worse when an epidemic like cholera or typhoid strikes the slums. I have lost two children from the program so far: Alawi and Mukasa. Alawi died of a mysterious disease that made his skin turn very rough and dark for months, whereas Mukasa was hit by a speeding motorcycle and died on the spot. Alawi's death prompted me to create rapport with the medical fraternity in the community, especially those who run private medical clinics. The idea is that the children in the chess program can be attended to in the event of an emergency, even when there are no funds. The bill is cleared later. This has been enormously helpful for the children. Several of the kids have been involved in bicycle and motorcycle accidents, including Brian Mugabi, Phiona's elder brother, who was involved in a hit-and-run motorcycle accident that nearly claimed his life, as portrayed in the *Queen of Katwe*. With such collaborations with the private health sector, there is a bit of assurance of medical attention to the learners in the program. It's my dream to establish a medical center for the program and for it to be operated or run by the children who have been trained in the medical field, such as Samuel Mayanja. This will not only create jobs for them, but it will also generate some revenue for the program as well as meeting the health needs for those children in the program.

"It always seems impossible until it's done."

– Nelson Mandela

CHAPTER SIX

HAVE A DREAM

The EIGHT-PLUS YEARS I spent at Auntie Jacent's home in Namasuba was a mixed bag of ups and downs. However, I set my mind to make the most of every opportunity that I received, especially what I considered vital for my personal development. I worked to consciously endure anything that came my way and tolerated every harsh treatment I was exposed to—especially by young Jacent, who waged a war between us because I was a threat to her favors from Auntie Jacent. She would deliberately make me miss meals, and at times she would drop a cockroach in my tea whenever it was her turn to serve breakfast. Of course, it was always worse whenever Auntie Jacent was away from home. So, I simply ignored whatever seemed unfair to me. Still, it was so hard on me that I would often feel my spirit burning with rage. But there was nothing I could do because I couldn't afford to be homeless or miss my education. In a way, the situation taught me tolerance. That is something I learned from Jacent—there had to be something to learn from the cruel girl's actions beyond the irritation they presented. I had seen and experienced far worse things than the provocations of a cruel schoolgirl.

Even still, it seemed that this was the straw that broke the camel's back, so to speak. Out of everything I had endured, her constant jabs were what began to awaken suicidal thoughts within me. I couldn't have lost my mother and been invited to live in Auntie Jacent's home—an invitation that was intended to fulfill my mother's death wish—just to be susceptible to endless needling. There had to be more; a bigger reason and a purpose to it all. This home was supposed to be a refuge for me; a resting place from the chaotic past of the village and ghetto. Perhaps I was wrong about that assumption, but the question then was: *When was I supposed to finally arrive in that place where I could live happily and be able to express myself like a normal human being? When?*

I have trained myself not to blame anyone in my life for the things I've endured. I have taught myself to think of what I need to learn from any kind of mocking because I firmly believe that everything God allows our way has a lesson in it. I have come to realize that good people bring happiness, bad people give experience, the worst people give a lesson, and the best people give memories. This is an attitude shift that has come in handy more times than I could try to count.

Throughout these experiences, I've learned that to succeed in life, you actually *need* enemies. Yes, you read that right! You need people who will mock you so that you can grow emotionally and learn to run to God. You need people who intimidate you so that you can learn to be courageous. You need people who will say "no" so that you can learn how to be independent. You need people who will disappoint you so that you can learn to put your hope solely in God, and not in people or circumstances. You need people who will frustrate you and keep you on edge so that you don't take it for granted and become passive. Or sometimes, it can go to the extreme—you lose your job, and positivity leads you to start your own big business. What appears to be an adversary is often our greatest benefactor.

I have frequently used stories to teach and mentor my learners as well as in my counseling services. The story of Joseph in the Bible is one that I've used often; it prepares and empowers us to cultivate a positive attitude towards harsh treatment. It teaches us to persevere in unfavorable circumstances. You need people who will sell you as a "Joseph" so that you can get to Egypt and be a Prime Minister in a foreign land of captivity. You need a cruel landlord so that you don't get too comfortable in someone else's house. We can see

Chess Strategy: Weigh Your Options

Chess gives us options, so we must always search for the best move possible, training ourselves to weigh each move.

Life Lesson: Find the Lesson

Improve your circumstances by mining the lesson to be learned in each situation. Then, you have options.

Nuggets of Wisdom

1. When you get, give; when you learn, teach
2. Always approach the game with a student's mind; there is always something to learn
3. Focus on where you want to go, not where you currently are
4. Have a plan, but be flexible

"What moves men of genius, or rather what inspires their work, is not new ideas, but their obsession with the idea that what has already been said is still not enough."

- Eugene Delacroix

"If you limit your choice only to what seems possible or reasonable, you disconnect yourself from what you truly want, and all that is left is a compromise."

- Robert Fritz

through the story of Joseph how important it is to look at life as a test or a puzzle because we tend to find ourselves in some pretty hostile circumstances. Life's challenging moments are inevitable. When we are disappointed, we tend to remain in a place of hopelessness. However, what we do not see in the moment is that the endpoint of disappointment is often the beginning of your greatest accomplishments.

I remember exactly how it felt when my mum passed on. Losing a loved one is an unavoidable part of the human experience, but still, no one can prepare you for the amount of grief it causes. Years later, I realized that this loss is what led me to break away from the slum life. When Auntie Jacent took pity on me and fostered me in her home, this also presented its own challenges that eventually made me the person I am today. Just as we find in the book of Romans, all things always work together for the good of those who love the Lord.

Don't get me wrong; it is definitely not easy to see the good in oppressive situations as we are experiencing them. It takes a certain level of maturity to adapt to this kind of attitude. Whenever I encounter a difficult situation, I ask myself the following questions: Why has God allowed this to come my way? What is the lesson for me in this situation? Remember, every situation will be turned around for good. You cannot see a new opportunity while you are still focused on the old one, spending all your time and energy trying to force an outcome.

Again, let me remind you: No challenge will ever come your way without an attached blessing. So, when the hard blows come, surrender the situation to God and thank Him for it. Tell Him to open your mind and spiritual eyes to see the new blessing that He has for you. Disappointment must come first in order for something better to present itself in our life. That is why it is called breakthrough: Something must break so that you can go through!

There are lessons to learn in every situation, be it good or bad, but it takes an inner power to harness the requisite positivity. Focusing on the big picture has enabled me to painfully endure many things. In the end, it comes down to your mindset; if you train yourself to recognize the difference between where you are now and where you wish to be, you can develop a stream of ideas moving forward. It is always the uncommon pain that gives birth to uncommon ideas. All innovation is a result of addressing a particular problem or alleviating a specific pain. I have learned never to allow the unfavorable circumstances I go through to define my identity or destiny. You belong where you wish to belong, not where you are currently. I refused to live an apathetic life and instead taught myself to handle every challenge as it came. Meanwhile, I focused on the bigger goal for my life, which was education.

Many times, I envisioned myself arriving at the front door of my very own home, my family and children running toward me to welcome me. I am driven by dreams and aspirations. While it may be true that everyone dreams about the future to some degree, not everyone is a dream *achiever*. Achieving your dreams takes a willingness to work hard to make it a reality by embarking on a journey of unlocking your potential. The process might be tough, filled with challenges and disappointments, but it is worth it.

Chess: Play the Middle Game

Be in control of your game by putting your pieces on good squares. Don't hold back too much, and don't push through too early. Your opportunity will come.

Life Lesson: Imagination is the Key

Imagine what you want to achieve, then make a plan.

Nuggets of Wisdom

1. We can't give away what we don't have
2. Self-confidence builds self-worth
3. Recognize your abilities and rely on them

"Imagination is more important than knowledge. For knowledge is limited, whereas imagination embraces the entire world, stimulating progress, giving birth to evolution."

— Albert Einstein

"Throw your dreams into space like a kite, and you do not know what it will bring back, a new life, a new friend, a new love, a new country."

— Anaïs Nin

Stimulating the Imagination

One of the greatest gifts to mankind is imagination. We must agree that every living and non-living thing in this world owes its existence to the imagination, whether that of God or humanity. Let's think of this in terms of yourself: The clothes you are currently wearing were first an idea in someone's mind. Think about the shoes on your feet, the chair or couch you are sitting on, the bed you sleep in, the car that you drive, and the building you live or work in. We can go on for weeks enumerating the things in the world that surround us, but in the end, we cannot escape the fact that it is imagination at work in every single one.

Imagination has been likened to daydreaming or dreaming while in the conscious state. Daydreaming is not any less credible than dreaming while we are asleep. In fact, more often than not, we forget our dreams as soon as we wake up or only recall hazy details. This is not the case with daydreaming; you are instead fully aware of what is running through your mind. Dreaming while you are awake embodies the whole essence of visualizing your future destiny. The ability to visualize your future grants invaluable motivation to pursue your dream as though you already have it.

All the created objects we see or have are nothing more than manifested visualizations. That shoe or shirt you are wearing is someone else's dream come true. The designer consciously dreamed about it and eventually added form to his imagination. That is the quintessence of creativity. For those familiar with the Bible, one of the most profound statements in the New Testament book of Hebrews is the definition of the term "faith." It is described as "the assurance of things that are hoped for; the evidence of things that cannot be seen." (Hebrews 11:1, KJV) In the scientific and legal realms, this statement can pass for the incoherent ramblings of an insane person because, in these disciplines, everything is premised on the law of evidence. But in the world of imagination, all things are possible.

Considering the above expositions, we can understand that every individual is limited by his or her own imagination. Then statements such as "wealth and/or poverty is simply a state of mind" begin to make sense to us. This explains why so many highly educated folks who are full of worldly knowledge are only able to get by and lead an average life, while the less educated ones who apply their imagination (call it wisdom) are able to scale the heights of success in business, creativity, and innovation.

Many of the wealthiest people in the world cannot boast of having a university degree. At least in my country,

Chess Strategy: Build a Team

Learning to make your pieces work together as a team is fundamental.

Life Lesson: Become a Team Player

Practice patience and consideration for others; knowing everyone has something to offer.

Nuggets of Wisdom:

1. Recognize the value others bring and leverage their talents toward a common goal
2. Appreciate diverse thinking and reasoning
3. Respect diverse perspectives
4. Improve your emotional intelligence
5. Practice forgiveness

If you don't have a goal, it's hard to make the right decision (or even know if you've made the right decision) with the information that's in front of you.

"Great leaders can see the greatness in others when they can't see it themselves and lead them to their highest potential they don't even know."

– Roy T. Bennett

Uganda, that is the case. Otherwise, Ph.D. holders would be the richest people in the world. But somehow, they become content to merely throw around their intellectual weight at the expense of imagination, thinking they have it all. Even some of the world's greatest achievers are not known to have completed their first university degrees. Bill Gates dropped out of Harvard and co-founded Microsoft in 1975, only to then become the wealthiest person in the world. The lack of a degree didn't slow Gates' rise to the top echelons of business. According to the *StatCounter Global Stats reports*, as of September 2017, hundreds of companies manufacture hundreds of thousands of brand-name personal computers each year, but most of those machines use Microsoft's Windows operating system. Microsoft went public in 1986, and by the next year, the company's soaring share prices had made then thirty-one-year-old Gates the world's youngest self-made billionaire. He has since been labeled "Harvard's most successful dropout."

Bill Gates is certainly not alone in this. It is said that the Macintosh computer, iPod and even Buzz Lightyear likely wouldn't have existed had Steve Jobs stayed in school. The future wizard of One Infinite Loop dropped out of Reed College after just six months because of the undue financial strain it placed on his working-class parents' savings. He would go on to eventually found Apple, NeXT Computer and Pixar, becoming an instrumental force in shaping the landscape of modern culture. The same story is true of Frank Lloyd Wright, America's most celebrated architect, who spent more time designing colleges than attending them. He was admitted to the University of Wisconsin-Madison in 1886, but he left after only one year. By the time of his passing, Wright's resume included more than five hundred works, the most famous of which are the Fallingwater, and New York City's Solomon R. Guggenheim Museum.

Break Goals into Small and Manageable Tasks

The ability to devise a strategy and break goals into small and manageable tasks with proper timelines is one of the greatest skillsets on which I rely. In most cases, I may not have what it takes to achieve my dream, but realizing where I need to start and what steps I need to take gives me the tools I need to see my dream realized. It will require much patience and perseverance, but at least now we have a step-by-step process.

Setting a long-term goal is an easy, albeit vague, way to plan your life. For example, you know you want to lose weight or pay off a debt. However, if you truly want to reach those goals, you need a plan for how to get there. Goals aren't achieved overnight; they take planning, hard work and tenacity.

Kris Gellci, CEO of productivity app Handle, explains that setting a goal is a bit like deciding to climb a mountain. You know you want to get to the top, but that's pretty much all you have. If you're going to reach that summit, you need specific steps to get you there. After you've chosen a goal, plan the specific steps you need to take to achieve that goal. Once you have your plan, the only goal that matters is the next step.

When you start to work on a task that propels you toward your larger goal, place all your focus on that task alone. Don't check your email for a minute or look to see if there is anything interesting on the front page of Reddit—these are seemingly little things that quickly waste your time and throw you off task. You will get tasks done much more quickly and make more progress on your goal if you set a timer and avoid any context switching while the timer is running.

Once you get started, it seems a lot less overwhelming with a plan in place. Most of us don't have a hard time setting a goal, because it's easy to imagine what we want in life. Planning, on the other hand, is the hard part. Once you have a plan in place, though, you can break down your goals into tasks that are manageable every day.

"If you are planning for a year, grow rice. If you are planning for twenty years, grow trees. If you are planning for centuries, grow men."

– Guan Zhong

CHAPTER SEVEN

FOSTERING A CULTURE OF MENTORSHIP

ONE OF THE most frequently asked questions from those who know me is: "What compels you to do what you do?" Some have even gone a notch further to label me a modern-day "saint" in consideration of the work I do to better the lives of the less privileged. I choose not to take these comments as flattery or mere compliments, but rather, I view them as a glimpse into how far we've strayed from true compassion. I believe these statements are symptomatic of how low society has set the bar in regard to being "our brothers' keepers," as the Bible so beautifully puts it.

Contrary to popular belief, I don't think I am under any sort of compulsion to do the things that I do. Perhaps it is the wrong choice of words by those who seek to know. What I cannot dispute, however, is the fact that I have tried, to the best of my ability, to give my all in service to others. But again, it is not easy to say such things about oneself without risking being misunderstood or have the words be misconstrued as self-aggrandizement. Such is better said by other people.

Everyone desires to be well and have access to all they need (and at times what they *want*), but the heart, it seems, will never be satisfied with things. Living in scarcity is like living in captivity, but to be able to overcome it so as to become a blessing to others in return is a great achievement—one of the greatest, in fact.

Most of us will intrinsically teach other what we've been taught. However, it takes it a step further to fully commit yourself to making someone else's life better. Though some would imagine that pouring out your life could be a heavy burden, I would argue that in my case, it has been quite the opposite. I can assure you that this commitment is one of the most rewarding and gratifying things you'll get to experience this side of heaven. It is, indeed, satisfying—not because someone will say "thank you," but because you do what needs to be done without expecting anything in return. Often, I have been snubbed by those I serve (even though some of them eventually atone). I have come to learn that these are some of the experiences that grow our degree of tolerance.

Everyone has their own type of mission that they get completely engrossed in; the kind that yields an inner satisfaction that not even money can purchase. I personally delight in giving a hand to others who need to be pulled up. Being driven by a deep inner love, which is not just a *feeling* but a *commitment*, leads to devising all means possible to help out, even when there seem to be no obvious options to do so. This process is a true source of joy for me; it is actually more of a blessing to me than it is to the person I'm helping!

It brings me profound joy and gratitude when I see children developing and growing under my stewardship and guidance as a mentor.

If I had to answer the question that many people usually ask themselves before they do anything, "What's in it for me?" I think I would say that I am blessed to be a blessing.

As selfish as that question seems at first glance, nearly all of humanity has the same attitude: avoiding doing anything that has no reciprocal advantage. This simply comes down to what motivates us. Workers are motivated by a medley of factors: getting a raise or promotion, receiving compliments, qualifying for bonuses and a host of other strategies employers use. This motivation, however, is not free. But what the employer knows is that a motivated workforce will guarantee higher returns for the establishment that can easily plough back what was spent on incentives. Which means the employer first asked him or herself the same "What's in it for me" question before making the move.

The whole thing speaks of a chronic cycle of selfishness. If you ask me, I can truthfully answer that my primary motivation derives from seeing someone being uplifted from a place of misery to a place of significance.

Models of Excellence

Creating a culture of excellence can cause you to look to yourself as your own role model. For many, their role models are the beautiful faces that are plastered on beauty magazines— movie stars, pop idols or sports heroes. Somehow, we have mastered the thrill of projecting ourselves onto other people; we are content to live in the shadows of the looks or achievements of others. Their wins or losses becomes ours.

Millions of people are caught up in this fascinating fantasy world of quick and easy gains. Life has become reduced to a lotto. We count the days to the next lucky draw and continue to imagine winning millions. I believe in miracles, but I also know that we cannot always live on miracles. It is possible, therefore, that you are not presently what you were originally created to be, because of laxity and not doing enough to be at your best. Instead, you are a product of various outside influences you have come in contact with or have read about and watched on the big screen. This happens if your life has been lived from outside your means rather than from reality. You cannot find true excellence and fulfillment in what does not originate from your inner man.

We attach much value to the applause and recognition of our fellow man. Exceptional performance makes you public property. Yet the same crowd who praises you today would more than likely crucify you tomorrow, should the impression of the performance fade, disappoint or fail. Moreover, disappointments from our heroes can potentially leave us devastated and shattered because we had so much faith in them—more faith than we have invested in ourselves, even. In the end, putting your blind confidence in other people rather than yourself is not favorable for anyone.

We all have people we admire and look up to for inspiration. While interviewing people that have made it in any field, be it sports, entertainment or politics, one of the most frequently asked questions is, "Where do you draw your inspiration from?" In response, the subjects of the interview will usually talk about someone (or some people) who mentored them in their specific area of influence. Furthermore, these mentors could be someone they met with in person or someone they've looked up to from afar and learned from without ever meeting them in real life.

In many cases, the people we would love to be our mentors may not be willing or able to mentor us. However, that does not have to stop you from learning valuable lessons from them, albeit from a distance. I have been the beneficiary of many mentors who have shaped my life into what it is today. This enables me to have a strategy of studying and following those I admire. I have vowed to never miss out on an opportunity to ask them a question that I think would help take me to another level. Usually, I seek to know how they got to where they are. All humans, regardless of social or economic status, have both strong and weak points. In our interactions with those we look up to, it is good that we seek out the positive elements in each other and emulate them. But there is also something to be said about learning from someone else's mistakes as well. Either way, I look to all people for inspiration; some are people in high places, while others are my peers.

If you desire to both be mentored by and to mentor others, who you allow in your life is of utmost importance. "Don't be deceived, bad company ruins good morals." (1 Corinthians 15:33, ESV) I am always careful to keep my conduct in check, knowing well that even as I seek out role models to emulate, many others are looking up to me for the same. A slip up in character on my side could be seen as a form of betrayal by those who constantly look to me for guidance. I carry a huge responsibility on my shoulders every single day of my life. Ralph Waldo Emerson once said, "Your actions speak so loud, I cannot hear what you are saying." Along the same lines, William J. Toms said, "Be careful how you live, you may be the only Bible some people ever read." Both of these quotes should inspire us to be on our best behavior, and through that, hopefully, we can help others.

I have mostly used the principles I derive from my own life experiences to guide and inspire my learners to achieve. Chess has served a significant role in teaching life principles in relation to the game. The concept is to inspire them to succeed by being the best they can be in their endeavors as I walk the entire journey with them. They get to learn firsthand how I plan, approach and execute work and, above all, the reasons behind what I do. My learners know that my home is always open for them. In fact, I often take them to stay with me at my small house as one of the mentorship strategies. This helps them learn how a family setting should be, and helps prepare them for their own future families. It's not that I know it all—I don't. However, what I do have, I give away freely.

One of the concepts I employ with learners is fourfold: a) I do as they watch, b) then I do as they help, c) then the time comes when they do as I help, and d) eventually they get to do as I watch. I have used this strategy for a while, and it has never disappointed—not even once. Soon, the mentorship process becomes more of a lifestyle than a conscious means of knowledge transfer. I don't go out of my way to tell them that, "We are now at such and such a stage of the learning curve," as it is all an organic process only known to me.

One of the principles in my chess programs is that each learner is required to be accountable to a fellow learner. This helps me greatly when it comes to the newcomers in the program. I ensure that they get attached to their peer learners, and in a way, this is the first level of leadership in the program. This is the same concept I used for Phiona Mutesi during her early days in the program. I asked Gloria Nansubuga, who was younger than Phiona, to teach her the game. On one hand, it humbled Phiona to learn from someone younger than her, and on the other hand, it increased Gloria's self-esteem, confidence and sense of leadership. I also thought that Phiona would bond easily with Gloria, as they were both girls. This proved to be a much better situation than placing her with the boys whom she had earlier provoked when she pulled Joseph's nose following an altercation during her first appearance at the Katwe Chess Academy.

This strategy of peer mentorship has been incredibly effective. I take this as the first level of giving; all it requires for my learners is to teach another person what they have been taught. Since they all know they will be accountable to this system, they are very attentive while I am teaching and conducting sessions because they know that they will be required to pass the knowledge on. This also helps to set up leadership structures among them and help them stay accountable to each other (and their leaders). This methodology and concept apply even in the teaching of life skills and principles which constitute a very integral part of the SOM Chess Academy programs. Above all, we choose to enlighten ourselves using any opportunity that unfolds in front of us.

As another facet of the mentorship process, I match boys with boys and girls with girls and charge the entire group to be responsible for one another as members of one family. This pairing has worked out well for those who have gotten a chance to go to school; in fact, you can hardly tell that the students are not related by blood. They have built strong, unbreakable bonds among themselves. It is a responsibility taught and practiced at the Academy to be mindful of the wellbeing of each other, in addition to managing their personal lives well. I desire to see a community that is there for each other, doing their best to advance and pulling one another up to do it together. In this process, the game of chess has granted us an invaluable platform to think and devise solutions for managing our lives, even in the midst of scarce resources.

As mentioned earlier in this book, I literally did all manner of work at home as a child: looking after chickens, cows, slashing the compound using a hand slasher, fetching water, washing vehicles, cooking, washing clothes and some-times even washing my uncle's underwear! Of course, I had to put up with the torment from some of the older children in the house on top of it all. I didn't care much; as long as I was fed, sheltered and had the opportunity to attend school, I would gladly endure anything that came my way. Doing the hard work nurtured me into building a selfless working character, and I always focused on accomplishing my tasks in the most timely and practical way possible.

My work ethic also granted me some favor at home. Favor in my life has been like the currency to help me see the next day, and by far my greatest bargaining chip. Obedience, servanthood and living selflessly became my immediate goals in life. My willingness to give a hand, even at school by helping my fellow students, became my lifestyle and the favor that accompanied this service gave me a sense of belonging. It is obvious that favor is worked for—behaving well and doing what is expected of you (and beyond) yields extraor-dinary results.

Ultimately, the main content of my mentorship derives from the various personal experiences already enumerated in this book. I have not had to struggle much to make textbook references to lessons, given that my history is already full of countless lessons that apply to the learners' prevailing situa-tions. In the same vein, I also encourage them to use their life experiences to share knowledge with their peers whose chal-lenges are usually similar. The beauty of this concept is that these children will never be able to get this knowledge from the school's academic curriculum. As they say, "experience is the best teacher!"

"You never know what's around the corner.
It could be everything. Or it could be
nothing. You keep putting one foot in front
of the other, and then one day you look
back and you've climbed a mountain."

- Tom Hiddleston

CHAPTER EIGHT
FINDING A POSITIVE ANGLE

GROWING UP WITH very little allowed me an advantage when it comes to work ethic and perseverance. The fact that I had next to nothing in terms of resources helped me to cultivate a positive attitude towards work—I knew that if anything was to happen, I had to be the one to figure out the way. I had no parents to help me out, and no close relatives to place my hopes in or rely on. So, I had to instead rely on God as my sole source of comfort and resources, and I had to build up my strength and abilities to endure wherever I was. I knew all about survival of the fittest. However, even in this survival mode, I learned a valuable life lesson: There is always a positive angle to be found in any situation. I believe this is where the scriptures assert that all things work together for the good for those who love God. Knowing His purpose for our lives helps guide us to His will, and even that which was intended for evil gets turned around for good.

For example, there were many times when I did my domestic chores with an eye on improving my physical fitness, particularly whenever I had an upcoming football match at school. I would run the three-kilometer distance to fetch water for home use, trying to beat my previous time as if it were a race. I would give myself deadlines for accomplishing different tasks, treating everything as if it were a game where I was to do everything I could to win.

No one could ever figure out what it was that motivated me to work so efficiently. In fact, they may have perceived me as nothing more than a suffering boy sidelined by his hosts. They probably thought I was just a hardworking "machine" by nature, but because I wasn't allowed time for training, I had to find creative ways to keep myself physically fit to compete favorably at school football games.

There are certainly many luminaries all over the world who have walked down this familiar path of turning their trials and tribulations into resounding testimonies.

Haile Gebreselassie is an Ethiopian athlete who is considered by many to be the greatest long-distance runner of all time. He has two Olympic Gold medals in the 10,000m category. He has won the Berlin Marathon a record four times—two consecutively. He has won the Dubai Marathon three times, as well as the 2001 Half Marathon. He has broken sixty-one Ethiopian records in distances from 800m to 26.2 miles. He also has twenty-seven *world* records, ranging from 1,500m to 26.2 miles.

I'm sure after reading of his accolades you are likely thinking this is one lucky fellow. However, I believe that Haile's success isn't just luck, but hard work. Just as Louis Pasteur put it, "Fortune favors the prepared mind."

The Ethiopian discovered his talents by default rather than by design. He did not intrinsically have any interest in running, but while he was still young, his poor parents sent him to school some twelve kilometers from home. It was the closest school in proximity, so there was no choice. He had to jog the distance from school to home for years on end. It turns out he was so fast that his friends were never able to keep in step with him. This, of course, is a significant burden for a pre-teen child to endure. No one to talk to for twelve kilometers?! Surely no parent would wish to subject their son to such daily misery.

However, what started out like a punishment would later vindicate them. This "punishment" would propel their son into the limelight and lift them from the abyss of poverty for good.

After enduring the distance for some years, running soon became like second nature to him. He easily made the school marathon team. His talent was quickly spotted, and he was asked to run for the Ethiopian

Chess Strategy: Consider Broadly

Always consider the whole board when deciding on a move: decisions made with too narrow a focus are often bad.

Life Lesson: Train to be Your Best Self

To experience the best wins in life and business, confidence will be your secret weapon. It will give you the fuel to take the next shaky step and trust that God will provide a net to catch you. But your confidence levels are dependent upon how prepared you are. Train to be the best at what you do.

"Achieving in life is not just being in the right place at the right time but also being in the wrong place at the wrong time and not giving up."

– Philip Baker

national athletics team. Without any training, this boy from the hills was able to run faster than many of his trained teammates.

He matured into a global icon, winning in all manner of world championships for years on end. His outstanding record could never be attributed to sheer luck or good fortune. Instead, it was the result of tremendous good being worked out of a situation that was less than ideal. It was the result of enduring the seemingly harsh run to and from school. You may say that circumstances could have contributed to his talent discovery, but you should also know that he had the option to give up school because of the harsh environment, just like many of his ilk do all over the world. The power to act is essential in the realization of dreams. You can choose to be inspired by adverse conditions rather than be dissuaded, depending on your attitude towards negativity.

The intersection between the story of Haile Gebreselassie and mine is that we both didn't end up working in the professional lines that the education system had prepared us for, but instead were shaped by our childhood training as occasioned by harsh circumstances. This echoes the quotation that states mishaps are like knives that can either serve us or cut us, depending on how we hold them—either by the edge or by the handle. Had Haile's school been a stone's throw from his home, there is a fair likelihood that he would have nothing to do with the sport. He would probably be working at a desk job somewhere in an organization, civil service or doing business—certainly not dreaming of gracing the billboards in the stadiums of the world with his name and accolades highlighted. By the same token, had I lived a "normal" life as a child and gone through school with ease, the prospects of working with children in need would be a distant mirage.

I remember how I used to go to the village every Friday after school in Lubiri S.S. to work in the garden over the weekends. I would then carry food back home on Sundays that would take us through the entire week at Auntie Jacent's. I would either go to Mpambire on Masaka Road or Budaali on Hoima Road, depending on where I was sent. One weekend, I arrived in Budaali village on a Friday night, as was my custom. Very early on Saturday morning, I dashed to the garden. Little did I know that there was someone who had died in that village and their burial had been scheduled for that day. I saw people passing by one after the other, not knowing at the time that they were going to attend a funeral. I continued with my garden work for about two hours when I was interrupted by a group of men approaching me. They told me that the community chief wanted to see me immediately.

I asked them what the matter was, but they insisted that I had to oblige without question. I began to sense danger, so I obeyed and followed them along the path. On reaching the place, I saw many people gathered, both men and women. My first impression was that perhaps it was a community meeting, but when we reached the home, I was welcomed by a large crowd of people wailing and screaming. That's when it hit me that someone had died. It explained the masses of people that passed me by while I was busy tending to the garden. Feeling my anxiety rising, I immediately entered into panic mode. A cold sweat broke around my temples, and I knew I was in real trouble. I was forced down to the ground by my "captors," surrounded by a group of elders.

"Young man, how dare you work in your garden when we are mourning a community member," one of the elders said, his voice sending chills down my back.

"I assure you I had no idea about the death; I arrived last night..."

I tried to defend myself, but no one would have any of it. They seemed to be convinced that I violated the village norm: laying down work tools whenever the community lost a member. I was aware of the custom, and I certainly would never have headed to the garden had I known about it in advance. I knelt and pleaded for pardon, but no amount of petitioning could make them change their minds. I had committed a sacrilege in their eyes, and they insisted I did it intentionally. As my punishment, I was ordered to join the gravediggers and excavate three feet underground.

It was one of the most horrendous events of my young life, and as you've gotten to know my story, you know I've been through a lot! They were treating me as if I were a hard-core criminal who had committed a serious offense. I was the center of attraction in the large gathering, and I could see from the mourners' faces that they viewed me with spite and revulsion. They would have probably spit on me if they had the opportunity. I felt this was totally unfair to me; surely, I was innocent. I didn't recognize any faces in the crowd, and no one would come to my defense. At first, I thought they were joking, perhaps only scaring the daylights out of me and afterward would tell me to go, never to do it again. How wrong I was! I was dragged to the graveyard and handed over to a group of adults who had earlier started on the work. By now my eyes were welling up and panic had permeated my entire body—so much so that I was shaking like a leaf.

One of the men who took me from the garden told the others that they found me busy tending to the garden instead of joining the rest at the funeral. This news infuriated the men who were already visibly high on booze (and likely some other strange substances). They looked at me with disgust and hate and threw me into the pit. I was ordered to pick up the shovel and start scooping out the soil. By this time, I was sobbing loudly, unable to hold back the tears and fear. If only the people at home knew what was happening to me. They thought I was busy digging in the garden, and yet here I was digging a grave!

While I was busy working, one of the men poured alcohol on me and rebuked me. "Why are you crying?" he reprimanded me. "You are making noise for us; shut up!"

I obliged to their every command like a sheep headed for the slaughterhouse until they were satisfied.

That weekend, I was unable to do any other work. After finishing the grave, I had to hang around until the burial was done. I didn't know anyone in the community and had no way of communicating to Auntie Jacent. The first time I had gone to the garden with Auntie Jacent, she only showed me the land and the boundaries of the garden. She did not bother to introduce me to a single person in the community.

The same evening after the burial, I approached one of the elderly mourners to inquire if it was OK for someone to go to the garden and pick some food. She told me that there was nothing wrong with that—people have to eat in spite of the funeral anyway. Without wasting a second, I dashed to the garden, harvested some cassava, walked to the main road and boarded the next bus back home.

Upon my arrival at home, people were shocked to see me returning that day instead of the appointed Sunday. I narrated to them my ordeal, careful not to leave out any detail. I had assumed that they were all going to be overwhelmed by the magnitude of suffering I was subjected to and thus express some sympathy. Instead, it was me who was shocked because the story neither elicited any significant attention nor was anyone sympathetic toward me. I felt deeply disappointed, and even betrayed.

"Just how much hate could little me take in?" I wondered. I ran behind the house and shed some more tears, then composed myself and started on the routine work around the house. I was reminded of the Nigerian proverb that says, "Unless the wind blows, you will never see a fowl's rump." At the very least, thanks to this event, I now unequivocally knew how everyone felt about me.

*

I have come to understand that simply *having* an opportunity isn't enough; one must make good use of that opportunity. There is a degree of excellence in each one of us, but it requires determination, commitment, perseverance and endurance to make something out of it. In most cases, we try our best to work our way out of any hopeless situation by focusing on developing life skills and survival instincts while tenaciously holding on to hope in our hearts as one of the precious assets. It is this hope that enables us to hang in long enough to experience miracles in each of our lives.

Using chess as a platform for teaching and mentoring, several children are continuing to assume positions of leadership in different capacities at the time of this writing. Each one of them is being empowered in their respective fields of interest and ability. Ivan Mutesasira was among the pioneers of the SOM Chess Academy in Katwe. He joined SOM in 2004 when he was thirteen years old and had just completed primary (elementary) school. He dreamed of becoming a civil engineer someday, and it seemed as if it was going to stay that way: just a dream. His parents could not afford to pay his tuition to join high school, so he spent the year at home.

As he watched as other kids went to school, he couldn't help but think he would never be able to make it to school again. He was among the first twenty kids at SOM who could not play football, and still, he wanted to take part in the Sports Outreach activities. Remember, this was the same time we decided to bring on chess as part of SOM, so he was able to stay in the program. Sixteen of the kids ended up walking away from chess for various reasons, but Ivan stayed, along with six others: Brian Mugabi, Richard Tugume, Samuel Mayanja, Gerald Mutyaba, Benjamin Mukumya, and Julius Ssali. They soldiered on, playing chess every day, usually in the most inauspicious surroundings.

Ivan grasped things very quickly, and anyone could see that, given a chance, this young man had a lot awaiting him. That chance came when Ivan was selected to join the Sports Outreach education sponsorship program as its first beneficiary. He enrolled at St. Mbuga Vocational Secondary School. Ivan easily excelled in both chess and education in almost equal measure. He participated in several inter-school tournaments and won numerous medals and trophies. He eventually went on to join the team that represented Uganda in Sudan, along with Phiona Mutesi and Benjamin Mukumbya. The team emerged as overall victors in the competition and won trophies. This was the first major victory of the Katwe chess kids on the international scene.

Ivan went on to pass his Uganda Advanced Certificate of Education exams and was admitted on government sponsorship to Busitema University, where he studied a Bachelor of Science in Education, majoring in Physics and Mathematics. Although this was not his dream course, there was no choice because it is what he was given on government support. I encouraged him to take it on and, hopefully in the foreseeable future, he would still be able to pursue his dream course. In 2016, he secured employment at an international school in Tanzania to teach physics and mathematics, on top of conducting chess training programs for students. In 2017, he landed a rare opportunity to study Civil and Environmental Engineering at the Uganda Christian University in Mukono courtesy of an all-expense-paid scholarship from Sandra, an American friend of SOM Chess Academy and a missionary for many years in Uganda.

Ivan is a classic example of the success stories of Katwe and is a major inspiration for many youngsters who aspire to graduate from the slums of Katwe into meaningful adult lives. His perseverance in the Chess Academy at the time when things seemed bleak, when most of his colleagues found it convenient to walk away and find "better things" to do rather than waste time on a boring board game, eventually paid off. He cemented his place in the annals of the SOM Chess Academy in Katwe as the pioneer recipient of the Sports Outreach education fund, paving the way for scores of other children to benefit from the same. He was ready and able to see the bright side of things where others only saw darkness. This is an important ingredient of greatness, particularly coming from a youngster. This is the quintessence of finding a positive angle. Ivan is now among the instructors at the SOM Chess Academy in Katwe, where he uses his personal story to

Chess Strategy: Anticipate Obstacles

In the end game, attack the king by focusing your attention on his escape squares: when you are in the final stretch, and about to win, anticipate what could go wrong and plan accordingly.

Life Lesson: Unpredictability is Key

There is nothing more satisfying than a discovered attack: pretending to do one thing while attacking somewhere else. Learn to play and live less obviously and on more levels. This makes you less predictable and more interesting.

teach the young learners, encouraging them to focus and take every opportunity they come across seriously.

Many other kids were adept at picking clues from their predecessors—a thing that has seen several realizing their dreams. For instance, Joshua Semanda, who was one of my immediate leaders among the children, learned and became adept at bricklaying and now works with Omega Mansions Company, one of the biggest construction companies in Uganda. He now takes care of his entire family and also supports his friends who desire to study bricklaying as a course.

I once got a one-off gift of $1,000 from a friend named Allain Clenets as an incentive to support any child of my choice in school. I realized that getting to enroll a child in school with these funds would only cover two-and-a-half years. I decided to enroll 22-year-old Paul Mubiru, one of our emerging leaders at the time. Paul liked computers, so I had enrolled him for some computer vocational training. However, because he had not done sciences at the advanced level, no institution would allow him to take any of the courses. I advised him to pursue mechanical work as an apprentice—that way he would have an opportunity to sharpen his computer skills.

After a lengthy discussion with Paul and his mother, we agreed that I would send him to a mechanical workshop manned by my in-laws. I paid his tuition and bought him the requisite tools for the apprenticeship. The tuition would only cover one year. By the end of the period, he had attained several skills in motor vehicle mechanics. The company retained him for a while working at Gatsby Automobile Company, a training facility for students of mechanical engineering at the

Faculty of Science and Technology at Makerere University, one of Africa's most prestigious academic institutions.

Although he lacked the required academic credentials for enrollment, he did not disappoint in meeting the expectations of his instructors. He so far surpassed their expectations, in fact, that they kept him on as an important human resource. He later started to teach in an international school while doing the mechanical work. At the time of writing this book, he heads the computer lab at Kampala School for the Physically Handicapped in Mengo. He currently supports himself and his mother. They even moved away from the ghetto neighborhood and acquired a plot of land in Ndejje—Kikajjo, one of the fast-developing city suburbs. He also started a Chess Academy that now plays in the National Chess League. He is also venturing into agriculture, with an affinity for growing passionfruit. Amidst all this, he still volunteers his time as an instructor at SOM Chess Academy whenever there is an event.

Given my circumstances, getting an education was not guaranteed. Against all odds, I eventually managed to receive training in Civil Engineering and later in Information Technology, in which I earned a first-class degree that opened the door for me to become a junior lecturer at a university. I passed the interviews to lecture in Kampala University; however, considering the fact that it would come at the expense of my commitment to the children I was mentoring in the chess program, I opted to turn down the offer. I know that with the severe scarcity of job opportunities in my country, many young graduates would have gladly cut off their arms to take on this job. Not to mention I also felt the pressure to take the position because it would guarantee myself and my family an assured end-of-month paycheck.

However, my passion carried the day, even though it didn't promise much in terms of material gain. I instead chose to hold onto my teaching job at the high school, where I was helping to enroll the children from the chess program for formal education at a subsidized fee. I was deeply inspired to help these children in any way I could. I always felt peace of mind when I was with them discussing life challenges, encouraging one another and sharing the little we had. This turned out to be my day-to-day activity, and eventually became my occupation. It never crossed my mind that it would ultimately lead to an article in a magazine, a book or an award-winning movie! This confirms the notion to never despise the day of humble beginnings. Hundreds of children are now being empowered through this program and others are now professionals in the various fields, such as education, finance, medicine, accounting, information technology, and chess, to mention just a few.

CHAPTER NINE

THE JOURNEY OF GROWTH

I INITIATED A chess program in St. Mbuga Vocational Secondary School to not only enable the children to have a sense of belonging, but also to represent the school for the national competitions. I saw this as a worthy venture to invest my time in because the children would, in turn, create massive visibility for the school on the national scene. I had a strong conviction that each year the children would represent their school at the national schools' chess competitions. I also initiated the children's team to enable more children to participate, including those who were not attending school. I wanted to give them an opportunity to travel and compete at the national level.

All of this seemed to work perfectly well until it came time to talk about funding for the national championships. It was a nightmare. The school administration told me that they didn't have the funds and that their budget could not even foot the cost of registration of participants and their transportation to the venue. Knowing in my heart that this was something that needed to happen, I decided to find a way to take the children to the national chess championships myself. I requisitioned the Sports Outreach Ministry van for transportation, and they obliged. Next, I approached the school's director, Mr. Osborn Muyanja, who was also a close friend of mine, to make a personal contribution. I remember going to his home and presenting the request to him, shaking in my boots a bit. He was kind enough to give me 300,000 shillings (about $100 then) out of his pocket right then and there.

I managed to get enough money to be able to take two teams: the school team and the children's team from Katwe. We travelled over 80 kilometers to Jinja College School in eastern Uganda, the hosting institution for the tournament that year. The school and the tournament featured in the national dailies for the entire week, as well as appearing on all major media and sports news programs. We didn't end up winning the championship, but being in the media was a great achievement in terms of giving visibility and mileage for our teams. Riding on this achievement, I began to lobby for hosting rights of the subsequent National Chess Tournament the following year. After a protracted struggle, punctuated by some internal disagreements among the organizers, the slot eventually fell to us.

With only a month left before the tournament, St. Mbuga was selected to stage the games with some promises of logistical support. It was a huge relief on their side as much as it was a great favor for the school. That meant there was no need to foot transport costs for the school's chess team and the children's team from Katwe, as was the case the previous year. We competed favorably in the event, and we took the championship—the first time for a private school to win the

Father Grimes National Schools Chess Championship. We had made history!

This was just the beginning of countless victories that would open a new era of dominance by the school and children's teams, not only at the national but also at the continental level. Father Grimes was a British Catholic missionary and had been headteacher of Namasagali High School since the 1950s. He introduced chess in the school as a compulsory extra-curricular subject taught in class. This later led to the start of the National Secondary schools' competitions named after Father Grimes. It was no wonder Namasagali dominated the championships for decades. The trophy would eventually start to rotate among the famous government schools, and it was Mwiri and Namilyango dominating the championship. That was, of course, until SOM Chess Academy arrived on the scene to challenge their supremacy.

Chess Strategy: Recognize True Threats

Ignore meaningless threats and anticipate and deal with the dangerous ones swiftly.

Life Lesson: Laziness Threatens Success

Successful people use their time very wisely. They don't get sidetracked by people who are not on track, and they don't quit until the job is done. Laziness may appear attractive but will ultimately derail you from your end goal. Prioritize your life, identify what's most important and eliminate everything else.

"I believe that imagination is stronger than knowledge. That myth is more potent than history. That dreams are more powerful than facts. That hope always triumphs over experience. That laughter is the only cure for grief. And I believe that love is stronger than death."

– Robert Fulghum

Initially, the Father Grimes Chess Tournament was pitting two schools (Namasagali and King's College Buddo) against each other year after year because there was not much infrastructure and interest from other schools. The two schools would visit one another each year (although later other schools joined before it was taken over by the government). They had never before had a non-schooling team participate in the tournament until 2005, when I managed to convince the Uganda Chess Federation to include the children's team from Katwe in a championship that was held at Buddo Kings College. This was the start of several other developments and ideas that enabled the Katwe kids to dominate the Junior Chess in Uganda until they were merited to represent the country in the African Junior Chess program in Juba, Sudan. Their victory in Sudan interested several journalists, and they came to interview the kids straight away.

I remember the time I had to prepare Phiona Mutesi and her entire family for the massive opportunity of having a book written about them, and how their life experience was to be shared to the entire world. Although there wasn't any money attached to it, it still required psychological and emotional preparation because we could find ourselves in front of the camera or on some kind of panel for an interview. The preps became even more serious when I learned that Disney was intending to secure rights to the story and that there was to be a commitment fee that would be paid to us. Harriet, Phiona's mother, was selling eggplants in Kibuye market on the outskirts of Kampala City at the time, and her net capital in stock was less than $10. She could not even realize $1 as profit from a typical day's sales! I know this because I asked her what she would do with a surprise sum of money. In response, she said she would stock eggplants for her petty business and stop getting them on credit.

Furthermore, I asked her whether she knew of any of her colleagues in the same market who had been able to acquire a plot of land or build a house of their own with profits from their trade. She said she was not aware of any such people. The only success stories from Kibuye market were about those who had enough funds to own a stall. I was simply gauging her thinking about the possibility of owning a plot of land for her family and eventually setting up her own home.

The possibility of owning her own house was a very distant idea that felt like chasing a pipe dream at that time. It seemed like a mockery to her to even initiate such talk. She didn't own any identification, she had never had a bank account, she couldn't even write her name! Of course, this would turn out to be an important issue. In consideration of the prospects that were coming, I thought it was time for her to learn to, at the very least, write her name. I embarked on the task straight away. I encouraged her children to first help her to write, then make her copy the letters. They were to repeat the process until she mastered it. This is actually a common issue with all the families of the children who are connected to the Chess Academy.

Most times, I invest more time in the children than I do with adults simply because they are always yearning for information. I try my best to handle them individually to identify how best to empower them so that they also pass on the skills they have learned to others. It is mandatory for each one of them to teach what they learn to others, as I mentioned earlier. This helps them to concentrate during the sessions, as they are well aware that they have to pass it on. It also nurtures them into responsibility, no matter what age they are. It seems like there is endless information to learn and, at times, you wonder where to start. I try to simply handle one task at a time.

At this point, I am well aware that if a person tries to do everything, he or she may end up becoming a jack-of-all-trades and master of none. I try not to fall into the temptation to do everything before I establish and consolidate one. I am certain that a good approach is to first finish one task before you pursue another, especially if I anticipate that it could jeopardize the first one. I learned this idea from the way I teach chess: focus on handling one piece at a time, get it consolidated and then move to the next. You'll see this idea in our academy slogan: "Transforming Lives Through Chess One Move at a Time."

The ability to identify children's abilities/gifts and guide them on how to develop them is a fundamental element of my social work. I am well aware of the things that I am good at, and throughout my childhood, I felt like I could do anything once granted an opportunity. I also learned that no matter how many gifts you have, you shouldn't let them distract you. You need to concentrate on one or two gifts and stir them up. Don't worry about losing the other gifts. Decide on what you really want to do as a matter of priority and the other gifts will follow through. God will never put to waste that which He has given you. As earlier mentioned, trying to do everything is not good because you become a master of none.

"I said to my children, 'I'm going to work and do everything that I can do to see that you get a good education. I don't ever want you to forget that there are millions of God's children who will not and cannot get a good education, and I don't want you feeling that you are better than they are. For you will never be what you ought to be until they are what they ought to be,"

— Martin Luther King Jr.

The Discipline of Growth

They say that success is not always born in comfort and convenience but through sweat and blood. However, to attain an extraordinary achievement, one might have to go the extra mile; from inconveniencing your convenience to taking a break from the flow. It is always a lot easier to swim downstream; in fact, it's almost effortless because there is added leverage from the water. Doing the opposite, however, is a different dynamic that will require working at a different level of power supply and thinking. Moving against the current means all odds

Chess Strategy: Sacrifice as a Winning Tactic

Sometimes you must sacrifice in order to achieve a breakthrough. Material sacrifice in chess is regarded as tactical play. No wonder chess is considered to be 99% tactics.

Life Lesson: Follow Your Intuition

At some point, you will have to make very hard decisions, but if you learn to follow your intuition you will always know what is best for you. Life is not about winning or losing; it's about continual growth. Just as it is not about making income, but rather the impact made with your income.

"Swimming upstream is never simple and yet the more one does it, the more natural it becomes. Muscles are developed, new territory is reached and the joy of fulfilling our potential suffuses our life. Upstream is better, not worse."

— Philip Baker

are against you—you are swimming against the force of the water and all the objects it carries with it downstream.

But, the benefits of swimming upstream include strengthening of muscles and unlimited adventure. The important thing to grasp from this analogy is that it takes determination, discipline and commitment to venture out of the crowd into virgin territory. First, you will be lonely because most of your would-be company will be drifting along in the ease of downstream. Second, you will attract some distasteful comments from those in the flow, who will refer to you as an arrogant, ambitious jerk. All this is nothing compared to the multitude of dividends found upstream.

Even then, is it surprising that there are far fewer wealthy people than the poor majority? Of course, it is far more difficult to become rich than the opposite. You don't have to do anything to be poor. You can do all the easy things: sleep long hours, have no plan, sit there, walk around, etc. and poverty will come knocking at your door. Last time I checked, the statistics were mindboggling! Global inequality is growing, with half the world's wealth now in the hands of just 1% of the population, according to the World Inequality Report 2018 (Alvaredo at el 198)[1]This situation didn't happen by chance. Wealthy individuals donate their money and support other countries and still make more than enough for generations to come. Few people can replicate their journey because they are simply not ready to venture upstream.

Make no mistake about it—many good things can be achieved by going downstream—good things that many average people get. But therein lies the issue; it has been said

1 "World Inequality Report." *World Inequality Report*, wir2018.wid.world/.

that the enemy of best is good. It is very easy to be sidetracked by seemingly good things that one can settle for and forget their higher calling. I believe even the best can get better. Sometimes you need to free your grasp of the good things in order to create room for the better ones. It is not easy to forego a shiny opportunity, particularly when it comes at a time when you are desperate. It could be a job opportunity that presents itself at the point in life when you are deep in debt or have many pressing needs. You feel the urgency to set aside all your dreams in order to deal with the expedient. Before long, you have gotten yourself so firmly entrenched that coming out will take more than just putting in your resignation letter. Meanwhile, time keeps on ticking away.

These situations are all too familiar to the ordinary folks who live by the mercy of prevailing circumstances.

The story of my life ultimately revolves around the use of chess as a tool to discover and build life skills among the ghetto community of Katwe (and now around the country). I have taught chess to young people and children of all walks of life and used the precious lessons thereof to empower them. Even more importantly, the children have been able to discover these lessons by themselves on the chessboard. Not a single person who has undergone the SOM Chess program has remained the same. None. A random survey of the participants will prove this on any day. We learn that we cannot make any progress by remaining who and where we are. We must plan, develop ideas and strategize on how to execute them in order to realize both short- and long-term goals while valuing relationships. Irrespective of the struggles, we must keep swimming.

My worldview has changed a great deal over the years as well. I have developed a personal value system that transcends the here and now, and I have come to agree with Rick Warren's hypothesis that when you live in the light of eternity, your values change. You use your time and money more wisely. You place a higher premium on relationships and character instead of fame, wealth, achievements or even fun. Building relationships is the driver of the work that I do, and it will remain so for as long as I live. I have also learned that there are few ideal and leisurely settings for the discipline of growth. Making headway in anything requires a certain level of sacrifice and commitment.

I have also come to believe that life is much like a chessboard. And there is no doubt; chess is a metaphor for life. Learning and using it to train in life virtues is fundamental. Just as in life, time is one of the opponents in chess. If you procrastinate, you will lose the game. You must take a move to be victorious. Often you must lose hundreds of games before becoming a good player. My history is riddled with countless stories of losses of all kinds: loss of family, friends, happiness, joy, subjection to months of hard labor without pay, scorn, being reviled and much more. I have learned that there are times when a well-placed pawn is more powerful than a queen. I lived the life of a pawn for the greater part of my life, if you remember. Now, I spend my time working to change the mindsets of young people who have been relegated to being pawns on the chessboard of life by circumstances. Some of these circumstances are poverty or family trouble, but some of them are born into their circumstance like the differently abled children in our chess programs. I have witnessed several of these so-called pawns plot their way through immense opposition and become queens, knights, bishops or rooks.

Chess, as in life, is a game of strategy where you have to always think ahead of your opponent. Like David Cordover asserts, each move you make has an effect on other people. Each move causes your opponents to think, to react and then make a move themselves. Their moves are always influenced by yours. It teaches one to think outside the box (or even without a box). There are times in a game when your plans are foiled, and you need a creative solution to stay in the game. This is also a skill we need to practice over and over in life. Thinking outside the box helps you find solutions to problems in ways that others may not think of.

"Strategy without tactics is the longest route to victory. Tactics without strategy is the noise before defeat."

– Sun Tzu

If an opportunity arises, take it. Opportunities don't always arrive when we need them to, so when one is presented to you, don't wait. This principle is used in chess all the time. Your opponent makes a fatal mistake, and you notice it. Most chess games are won because of lapses in the opponent's camp. Chess is also about action. When there is a threat in chess, you take action—you make a move, a strong move at that. You don't want to let life pass you by without going after the things you want. If there's a problem in your life that's hindering you from making progress, you have to do something about it. If you stay idle and ignore it, it won't go away, and your life will pass you by. This scenario happens in nearly every chess match ever played; not only do you quite literally have to make a move to keep the game going, but if you want to win, you need a plan, and you need to implement it as soon as you can. Rather than letting fate dictate the outcome of your game and your life, you have the power to take action and determine your own results.

Onward with the World of Katwe

Before Katwe was flung into the global limelight, it had a hellish reputation, even in Uganda. Each time I introduced our team from Katwe during appearances at major national chess competitions, we would be greeted with raised eyebrows and snickers among the crowd. This kind of attitude always affected the young players and caused their self-esteem to suffer. I decided that part of the training program would have to include orientation in social etiquette. The places around Kampala City where the chess competitions were held were also usually the first place where the Katwe kids ventured out of the ghetto into "civilized" settings. This was evident during one of the national chess tournaments that took place at the 5-star Hotel Africana in the heart of Kampala City. Most of them had never come close to such magnificence in their lives; the beauty of the place, the large swimming pool, the food, were all marvels to behold.

> "To get something you've never had, you have to do something you've never done."
>
> – Denzel Washington

But the premiere of *Queen of Katwe* at Century Cinema located on the swanky Acacia Mall in the affluent suburb of Kisementi around Kampala was adventurous for most if not all people from Katwe Slums. It was a star-studded affair with Lupita Nyong'o. David Oyelowo, along with the entire cast of the movie, were invited to the ultramodern facility. They were going to be bumping elbows with Kampala's A-listers! During that season, I asked Disney to organize a community screening for the people who were featured in the movie as extras. The facility could only host 800 people. Over two hundred of them came from Katwe alone, while the rest were from other ghetto neighborhoods of Bwaise, Kawempe, Nateete and Kibuli where SOM Chess Academy has establishments. There were over eighty kids present from the SOM Chess project alone. I had to make branded T-shirts for the SOM Chess Academy, not just to distinguish our team but to help the children who did not have decent clothes not to feel out of place. Most of the kids had heard stories of London, and their experiences were nothing short of awe-inspiring. They took lots of pictures and were very proud of the incredible opportunity to be there.

Our very own Richard Tugume was the assistant casting director, following my recommendation to Disney. The local community had a rare opportunity to make windfall incomes that they could previously only dream of. The filthiest section of Katwe was cordoned off for the entire duration of the production, and owners of the petty businesses were paid quite a premium; rates that were far higher than their regular sales. The activities surrounding the movie came to impact not only the Chess Academy beneficiaries, but the entire Katwe community. As mentioned earlier in this book, many of the kids referred to in the book were now adults. Most of them took up roles as extras and were paid, while others received stipends for taking bigger roles in the movie. Although the book publication had no monetary rewards in and of itself, it eventually led to the movie project that benefited the entire community in ways we could have only dreamed of previously.

We were also blessed to take part in several screenings of *Queen of Katwe* in North American schools, churches and communities. What we didn't prepare for were the fans seeking autographs from Phiona and me! It was quite over-whelming at times. There were days where we would sign over three hundred autographs as people patiently stood in the queues waiting for their turn. We signed their personal copies of *The Queen of Katwe* book, DVDs of the movie and personal chessboards. Thankfully, Phiona had recently learned to write in cursive; otherwise, her autograph would have caught people off guard!

Besides Phiona, there has been a general change in the outlook of SOM Chess Academy because the outfit has gained international recognition. Now, we have all kinds of people seeking to lend some assistance to the center, such as donations of chess books, chess clocks, cash and service as volunteers. Other assistance comes in the form of scholarship opportunities for selected kids, such as the study opportunities at St. Mary's College Kisubi.

It has now been decades since first I set foot in the ghetto. The one thing that I know for sure is this: Katwe will never remain the same.

"The ultimate test of man's conscience may be his willingness to sacrifice something today for future generations whose words of thanks will not be heard."

– Gaylord Nelson

PART TWO
(Contributing Editor Nathan Kiwere)

LIFE AFTER *THE QUEEN OF KATWE*

A LOT OF what the world knows about Uganda is through the image portrayed in cinema. The 2006 production of *The Last King of Scotland* was filmed in Uganda, telling the story of former Ugandan dictator Idi Amin Dada. It featured Hollywood star Forrest Whitaker and a largely Ugandan support cast. The next big thing to happen in cinema was eleven years later, in a 2015 production of *The Queen of Katwe*. A great deal of hype was generated around the globe by both the book and the movie. Since the release of the film, quite a bit has changed, to say the least. Many lives have been transformed by the massive visibility of the Katwe ghetto. The children who were auditioned and acted in the movie have gone on to gain contracts to do TV advertisements. The real-life characters in *The Queen of Katwe* movie are now traveling all over the world being invited to speak at conferences. So far, the film is the only Ugandan production to be bankrolled by Disney, as well as featured on Netflix. This movie serves as a powerful metaphor for the resilience of the human spirit.

The pioneers of the SOM chess program have all seen their lives transformed as a result of the film. Robert Katende, the linchpin of the "chess kingdom" of Katwe, has been emboldened by the rapid developments of the SOM Chess Academy programs occasioned by the book and the film. Lupita N'yongo and David Oyelowo, the Hollywood stars who took key roles in the movie, have stayed in touch with Robert and supported the program on a personal basis, as well as advocating for the work of the SOM Chess Academy by connecting and asking people to support the vision. Several other well-wishers have joined the mission as well, offering up their time, knowledge and resources. Some individuals like Maria Hwang, Genie and Rich Graveline, Janine, Trish, the Reese family, the Clenet family, the Gardner family and many other individuals have come up to support this vision. Robert has since expanded the wings of his vision to cover other regions of Uganda, facilitated the setting up of the new SOM Chess Academy headquarters, and appointed some of the pioneers to take on different leadership roles.

Those who have worked closely with Robert Katende, famously known as Coach Robert, can attest to the fact that of the many adjectives that define him, humility occupies the top position. It would be practically implausible to believe that Robert can tell his story with the precision it deserves without the polite side of him watering down some significant details. Robert is characteristically hesitant to take credit for things he does, even when many seek to put crowns on his head. This does not come as a surprise, given the kind of life he has lived.

He tested the limits of misfortune in countless ways, seeking to end his life on more than one occasion following overwhelming episodes, but he always bounced back into the battle ring to face yet another even more devastating foe. He has experienced the most undignified situations and endured the most subhuman circumstances, despised by even those who have achieved nothing in life. Robert is no stranger to all manner of pain; for the greater part of his childhood and early youth, he underwent emotional ordeals of all kinds, and his body suffered excruciating pain occasioned by fractured bones, hunger, and various other ailments.

"You will only become what you are becoming right now. Though you cannot go back and make a brand-new start, my friend, anyone can start from now and make a brand-new end."

– John C. Maxwell

At this juncture of his life, Robert has good reason to celebrate. He may not yet be where he would like to be, but thankfully he is not where he used to be. It is not farfetched to postulate that his humility derives from his high sense of awareness about his past; what it means to live life on the edge. Robert works to mitigate the circumstances of young people are experiencing what he went through himself, constantly surrounded by reminders about where he came from. He has decided to dedicate his life to the suffering children (as well as adults) of the ghetto of Katwe in Kampala city and other underserved communities. Consequently, he has become a father to the fatherless, a guardian to the widows, a mentor to the lost and many other roles that we may never know or hear. Moreover, Robert refuses to play the hero, despite the overwhelming reasons for him to do so.

The purpose of the second part of this book is to relay the story of Coach Robert Katende in unequivocal terms, through the lens of an outsider. In a bid to create a more critical appreciation of the story of Coach Robert, it is imperative that the voices of some of the people whose lives have been impacted by this man are heard. This section is a result of the several interactions with the members of families that have benefitted from Robert's generosity over the years and those he has interacted with, both locally and on the international scene. These are the voices that are able to fill in the gaps and missing links, without which Robert's story would be incomplete. The section is also a result of close interaction between Nathan (who helped in the qualitative interviews and documenting them) and Robert, along with Robert's close family and friends. These investigations shine a light on the hidden angles of Robert's life, and thus bring his story full circle.

Unlike *The Queen of Katwe* book, this publication largely highlights the post-book/film life of Robert Katende and his beneficiaries. It is a selective scrutiny of particular aspects of his story as accentuated by the specific people impacted by him. Significantly, it casts a spotlight on the high points of the post-movie and book era, with details of the current status of some of the pioneer members of SOM Chess Academy. This serves to underscore the practical impact of Robert's efforts over the years; the testimonies of those that have successfully utilized the opportunities that he has cast their way, and those that are already creating a ripple effect by becoming of service to others.

"Most humans, in varying degrees, are already dead. In one way or another they have lost their dreams, their ambitions, their desire for a better life. They have surrendered their fight for self-esteem, and they have compromised their great potential. They have settled for a life of mediocrity, days of despair and nights of tears. They are no more than living deaths confined to cemeteries of their choice. Yet they need not remain in that state. They can be resurrected from their sorry condition. They can each perform the greatest miracle in the world. They can each come back from the dead..."

— Og Mandino

CHAPTER TEN
RESURRECTION FROM DEATH

ROBERT KATENDE COULD not afford to die. Literally. He, more than once, attempted to end his life, but couldn't raise enough funds to purchase a portion of rat poison with which he hoped to put himself to eternal sleep. There he would find peace and rest from the endless struggles in this world—or at least he thought. He had heard a familiar phrase many times already while attending funerals of his loved ones: "Rest in peace," as the men of the cloth would say on such occasions. He must have believed them to the letter, and so he thought that if such peace could only be found through death, so be it.

The only reason he is alive today is because of one thing: poverty. He had given up on life; it had become meaningless to him. A total liability. Not that he hadn't tried; just that he swam against the tide for so long that he had become so worn out. The battle to stay alive had squeezed out every ounce of resilience from his broken spirit; so much so that he had nothing left to keep trying to breathe, sit, stand up and walk. All the things that many people take for granted.

Robert resolved that not everyone had to take the path that he did and live the life that he led. While he is still alive, he is dedicating his life to pull people from the cliff and return them to a position of hope. He enables the resurrection of those who were on the brink of suicide, as well as the countless others walking around as dead bodies. However, it should be noted that this has not been achieved by taking the path of least resistance. As a matter of fact, it is an ongoing battle that is still raging during the publishing of this book and one that will likely continue for decades to come.

Around 2006, Robert made a decision that demonstrated his incontestable predisposition towards self-sacrifice in order to shoulder the burdens of others. He turned down job offers that would have benefited him and his family to lead a financially stable life. It was one classic case akin to the biblical inference of Jesus Christ laying down His life for His friends as the ultimate demonstration of love, as reflected in the book of John 15:13.

"The achievement of one's goal in life does not come at a discounted price. Many refuse to pay it. The super achiever, however, realizes that before victory there is a battle; before resurrection, a cross. You cannot have one without the other."

– Hellen Keller

As the saying goes, "Interest creates ability," Robert became more interested in being the best in everything he did, from home chores to garden work. He looked after the chickens, worked at his auntie's rental houses by digging pit latrines, and all manner of cleaning, not to forget washing vehicles. His diligence and perseverance brought him favors as he was usually referred to as a very hard-working boy.

> *"The pessimist complains about the wind. The optimist expects it to change. The leader adjusts the sails."*
>
> – ANONYMOUS

In 2005, Robert sought an unpaid teaching job at St. Mbuga Vocational Secondary School as a mathematics teacher, where he was ready to work as a volunteer staff. The school is strategically located near Katwe and proffers an excellent opportunity for the kids who live there. Robert's target was to enroll in the school with the view to influence the admission of the beneficiary kids of the SOM Chess Academy. He was offered the job, and for two years he diligently taught math in the candidate classes of Senior 4 and 6 without earning a penny. However, during that time, he was able to not only influence the admission of several kids in the program, but he was also able to teach some of them in their classes.

One of the kids was Ivan Mutesasira, whose story was already told in the earlier chapters of this book.

Ivan

Ivan notes that instead of vilifying them for their mistakes, Coach Robert always encouraged them to learn from them. It resonates with the adage that says, "When you lose, do not lose the lesson." This emboldened Ivan to aim even higher in his pursuits. Inspired by Coach Robert's achievement of studying at the university on a government scholarship, he too was determined to make it to the university, despite the popular belief that making it on government sponsorship in the lowly St. Mbuga school was like expecting a camel to pass through the eye of the needle. Fortunately for him, he was able to defy the odds and make it to the university on government sponsorship—the only one to succeed in doing so during that year. It was a norm-breaking achievement on all fronts that a kid from Katwe could make it to the university on scholarship. Such stories were unheard of in Katwe, which was viewed as the very graveyard for the wretched of the earth. When Ivan defied the odds and made it to university, this drew incredible jubilation from all over.

Ivan attests to having learned many invaluable lessons through his relationship with Coach Robert. For instance, he learned to be more principled in life by setting a personal mission statement and core values that help guide his life. Robert taught him that a true chess player is one who applies the board game principles in real life. This includes thinking about something before doing it, making the best of every move and planning and managing time, among many other life lessons.

He says that chess has caused a massive shift in his mindset. He is more focused and can clearly see where he is headed in life. He has also learned to put his trust in God, following the example of Robert, and to seek His guidance in whatever he does. They always pray and share the Word of God as part of the SOM chess program, and it has changed many lives. Ivan has also noticed that a lot of the things that they have been praying for over the years, such as chessboards, computers and scholarships, have been fulfilled under Coach Robert's watch. This has encouraged Ivan to believe that his own pursuits are not in vain. Most of all, he learned to take life as an extension of the chess game. He is so grateful to have passed through Coach Robert's hands, having reclaimed his life after that moment of hopelessness when Robert picked him from the abyss of despair years ago.

*

Coach Robert went on to teach at St. Mbuga for ten years on a part-time basis, during which time he introduced a chess club there. That means he was able to coach not only those interested in the game among the students' community, but most notably the kids from the Katwe Chess Academy, including Benjamin Mukumbya and the Queen of Katwe herself, Phiona. Within the first year of the chess club, they were able to register Gold medals from the National Chess Competitions. The school also rose from oblivion to be mentioned in the same breath as the elite of Uganda's schools in the local mainstream media.

> *"It's not hard to decide what you want your life to be about. What's hard is figuring out what you're willing to give up in order to do the things you really care about."*
>
> *– Shauna Niequist*

Katwe was a place where many of Kampala's "dead" people lived and worked. One of them who is supposed to be dead is Gertrude Nanono.

Gertrude

Gertrude's tragic life is partially documented in *The Queen of Katwe* book and also highlighted in the first part of this one. Hers was one of the most extreme stories Katwe could produce, at least among those that were discovered. She had gotten too accustomed to cohabiting with the nasty flood waters of Katwe in her dingy shack where she lived with her children. Their few belongings in the 3x3 meter shack that included a sofa, bed and other personal items were completely worn out from multiple stains and rot created by the waters. Like many in her locale, and indeed as Robert felt years back as a suffering youngster, suicide was a preferred alternative to this lifestyle. She could probably bear all of the discomforts of spending sleepless nights standing and lack of a dry place for her and the kids to lay their tired bodies, but the prospect of starving to death for lack of something to put in their stomachs was something she could not put up with. Disappearing from her family for three days and eventually returning to bid them farewell on her way to death—only to find the miracle of food that Robert had provided to them and thus reversing her decision—will forever remain permanently etched on her conscience.

During this interview, she revealed that she had neither experienced happiness nor been able to show a smile for years on end. Hers was a dark world where nightmares, tears and death were her daily bread. For the first time in decades, she could afford to light up her face when in December of 2017, she was able to sleep in her own house with her children, and on her own land. They were able to acquire the piece of land with some of the funds from her daughter's involvement in

The Queen of Katwe, and they were incredibly grateful. Then, with the money from the unrestricted (used as deemed necessary) donation from Wheaton College that accompanied his Otis Social Justice Award in 2017, Coach Robert decided to use part of the donation to build them a house where they happily stay now. It is a two-roomed house with a store, using solar for the lights and a water tank for harvesting rainwater. It took some time before she realized that all this was real; not just a dream that she feared she could wake up from some day.

Fortunately, this was not a dream, and indeed was not too good to be true. The fact that she will now live the rest of her life without a landlord ever knocking at her door demanding rent; that her children will be able to study and amount to something, all point to the fact that God eventually remembers His own, just like He did the children of Israel after more than four centuries in bondage in Egypt. It was difficult for Gertrude to find the words to adequately describe what Robert has done for her family. "He is a good father, very patient, would encourage all the kids to stay strong no matter what the situation was," she said as she labored to find the words.

Joan

Joan Nakimuli is one of Gertrude Nanono's daughters. She joined the SOM Chess Academy in 2006, while in Primary 3. She had a special distaste for chess because she saw it as a dull, boring game. Her mother had to apply force to get her to join. She was also persuaded by the free meal of porridge that she could not get at home but could only partake of on condition that she played chess. Over time, she slowly began to find interest, and as they say, the rest is now history. Every Saturday she joined her two siblings, Stella Babirye and Richard Kato, to go to the community market in Katwe and scour through crumbs of raw food from garbage left behind by traders to take home for cooking. They repeated this exercise every Wednesday in Kibuye market, within close proximity to Katwe. Although they were picking leftovers in a public market, this too was not easy as they had to fend off fellow "pickers" who were older and wanted everything for themselves.

Joan was among the four girls who remained at SOM to play chess following the breakaway of a large chunk of children who had run out of patience. She has since traveled to many parts of Uganda because of chess and participated in many chess tournaments since Primary 4, winning many medals and trophies in the process. She is even the 2017 Under 20 Girls' national champion! There are many of her gold-coated medals and trophies lining the floor of their living room, and the rest are kept at the SOM Chess Academy. She shared that they had stayed there from 2012 to 2017, when they relocated to their own house. At that time, she was joining Senior 4.

At the time of writing this book, she is enrolled in the YMCA institute pursuing fashion and design. She is very passionate about helping out other children going through difficult situations the same way Coach Robert has helped her.

Auntie Jacent

As seen in the first part of this book, Auntie Jacent was one of the biggest influences on Robert's life following the death of his mother. His fate hung in his mother's death wish of having someone to take care of her son and the willingness and ability of Auntie Jacent to fulfill it. Given her modest means, she took it upon herself to ensure that Robert received the incredible treasure of education. Despite the amount of time that has passed since, Auntie Jacent clearly recalls the time she picked up Robert from his grandmother's shack. She had seven orphans to take care of, on top of her own six children.

Auntie Jacent had to work together with the orphans in the gardens to get food for the family. She reminisces that Robert seemed to have understood the dire situation he was in, judging by the rate at which he worked. First, the long distance to school that he had to cover daily without breakfast was quite telling. He loved whatever he did, and he worked incredibly hard. When she could afford it, she gave him 200 shillings to buy juice and pancakes at school. "Robert was obedient, patient, and reserved," she recalls. "From what I could see of him at that time, I am not at all surprised that he is making it in life," says Auntie Jacent. "These days, he is the one who takes care of me, particularly the times when I am in need. I have only asked him for help once; usually, he comes out on his own."

The tables have since turned, and Robert is now making sure Auntie Jacent is taken care of. Besides financial assistance, he also encourages her as much as possible. Among the seven orphans that she took care of, it is only him and one other who remember to check on her. Now, sixty-nine-year-old Auntie Jacent still lives with her husband in the same house where Robert was brought up in Namasuba. All their children have since left and have their own families.

Harriet Nakku

The story of *The Queen of Katwe* would never have been without Harriet Nakku, mother to Phiona Mutesi, Brian Mugabi, Night Nantongo and Richard Buyinza. Her story has been told and retold in both the book and movie, and thus doing so in these pages would be rather superfluous. Be that as it may, hearing Harriet's love for the young man who raised her children and herself from the abyss of despair to relative privilege is one thing that cannot go unsaid. Harriet is just one person who has found her place among the desolate of the earth. She had already been isolated by the departure of her husband, who left for naught. The burden of caring for four children and losing one in the process was a very daunting one, to say the least. Without any skills to assure her of decent income, she settled for the petty trade of selling vegetables in the local market that she got on credit for lack of capital, and other trivial activities like many of her ilk in the Katwe slums. Her life turnaround came when her son joined the SOM Chess Academy, as did the whole family later on. Despite her ignorance about the game of chess and the prevailing rumors in the neighborhood about the alleged ill intentions of the people behind the project, she let her children attend, likely because she had no alternative.

The life that Harriet lives today has an uncanny affinity to that of Gertrude Nanono. She, too, still gets the feeling that she is in a deep slumber and that one day she will wake up to realize that she was always dreaming. She recalls how God used Robert to perform the miracles that she has witnessed over the last decade. Speaking from the comfort of her house in Bujuuko, about 20 kilometers west of Kampala city, Harriet, a devout Christian, likens her situation to resurrection from death, referring to the scripture that says, "I am the resurrection, and the life: he that believeth in me, though he were dead, yet shall live: And whosoever liveth and believeth in me shall never die." (John 11:25-26) The kind of life she now leads could only be given by God Himself, who remembered her after she had been forgotten by everyone. She also likens her present circumstances to having crossed the River Jordan into Canaan, the same way as the Israelites moved from bondage in Egypt to the land promised to them by God, according to the book of Exodus in the Bible.

She speaks very profoundly about the coach: "Robert is young, and yet he has the heart of a parent; he does not discriminate against people, [and] my family and his are now very much connected like we are relatives. He has been able to parent my children without any reservation and stretched his magnanimity beyond imagination." She believes that of all the people that have benefitted from Coach Robert, her family has benefited most. But the one thing that still confounds Harriet, and which she still believes is nothing short of a miracle, is Robert's ability to tame the ghetto kids of Katwe. She always viewed the children growing up in the slum as a lost generation nearly beyond redemption, owing to the awful circumstances they were exposed to on a daily basis. Not to mention the majority are now in their early and late teenage years—a turbulent phase for all young people. Moreover, Robert was able to cultivate discipline and self-control in them in ways that Harriet fails to comprehend, including her own children.

She reveals how once in a while she returns to the Katwe ghetto to visit the very spot where she used to sell her goods. While there, she declares that the God who was faithful enough to get her out of that place to her own house, will take her and her children even further. Every time she does this act, suddenly she has faith to believe that she has not yet "arrived," but this could actually be a precursor to greater things to come. Instead of the eggplants and maize she traded in, Harriet now has a poultry farm on her land from which she earns a regular income from sales she makes.

However, the unsightly scenes she encounters in Katwe—of people who are still trapped in the web of poverty and disease—break her heart and remind her of her old, bad days. She often cries and prays to God that one day they will also be remembered and be able to lead a good life. She has also learned that not all bad things are meant for evil, after all. She has come to believe that no situation is permanent and uses her example to encourage those who are still going through this to take heart and not to lose hope. She grows food and supplements the feeding program for the Chess Academy from her land every harvest season.

Concerning Phiona, Harriet appears to be both elated and apprehensive; happy because her daughter has made her proud and achieved the ostensibly impossible, the very things that the seemingly privileged pursue without success. Apprehensive because she desires that Phiona continues to walk in the fear of God and avoid making the mistakes that come with fame and wealth. Thus far, her prayers are still holding because her daughter has proved that the years of training under Robert were not in vain. The two are constantly in touch via telephone.

"'Impossible is Nothing,' it said. 'Impossible is just a big word thrown around by small men who find it easier to live in the world they've been given than to explore the power they have to change it. Impossible is not a fact. It's an opinion. Impossible is not a declaration. It's a dare. Impossible is potential. Impossible is temporary.'"

– Elna Baker

CHAPTER ELEVEN
AN INFINITY OF POSSIBILITIES

Sarah Katende

Sarah has been married to Robert since June 26th, 2010. When they first met, she was a volunteer worker at the School of the Physically Handicapped in Kampala, Uganda. Sports Outreach was renting their premises at that time. Sarah would occasionally help with some work at Sports Outreach while Robert and his team also engaged disabled children in their sports ministry programs. It should be mentioned here that not many women would relish being tightly knitted with the life of Robert Katende, owing to the many *encumbrances* about him. Robert's life was an already overcrowded world with many orphaned and needy children struggling for his attention at every turn. Most women want to have space and the undivided attention of their spouses. However, Sarah was a different kind of woman; it turns out that she had led a life that had a close affinity to that of Robert.

Sarah lost both of her parents while she was still young; her dad while she was only two, and her mum when she was twelve. The loss of her mum was the last straw that contributed to the dismantling of her life. From then on, her education was bankrolled by different people, at one point by an eighteen-year-old missionary. She maneuvered through the many impediments and completed her studies, graduating as a teacher. While completing her course, she was singled out by Pastor Richard Miro of House of Glory Church in Kanyanya, near Kampala, to head the Orphaned, Widowed and Needy (OWN) church project. She performed all the duties of the project single-handedly, including going into the community to mobilize and register beneficiaries, set up activities for them, select suitable candidates for scholarships and scholastic materials, among other duties.

She derived immense pleasure from this work, as she considered it payback for the generosity that she received following the passing of her parents. Sarah was no stranger to serving in the community of the underprivileged; her transition from the OWN church project to the School of the Physically Handicapped was a natural evolution of what she was already passionate about. More than that, meeting a man with whom she shared a similar life path was more than just a bonus; it was a potential marriage of opportunities, passions, and dreams.

It did not take too long before such opportunities presented themselves. Barely two months into their marriage, Robert invited Phiona Mutesi to stay with them in their two-roomed condo in Lungujja, which was near Kampala. Soon, Phiona was joined by Benjamin and Gloria; Benjamin slept on the couch in a sleeping bag while the two girls slept on the floor on the mattress. Despite the humble environment, all the children felt like they were in London in comparison to the horrid conditions from which they had been picked. This speaks of the nature of depravity that they had suffered, to the extent of thinking of sharing a mattress on the floor in a modest room as liberating.

Sarah considers the trio as the first children they had before their own biological children came into the picture. To Robert and her, they were scarcely any different from their own. To prove this, the youngsters were not there as mere visitors; Phiona went on to stay with them for a whopping seven years. Even after the construction of her mother's house, Phiona continued to stay with them instead of joining her mother and siblings. This living situation greatly helped her to learn from Teacher Sarah and be nurtured by a father figure in Robert.

The biological mother of Benjamin and Gloria mysteriously disappeared from Katwe, purportedly over too much debt and scarcity, leaving them behind with nothing. To date, Benjamin refers to Sarah as mum. As of the writing of this book, Gloria was busy nursing her HIV-positive auntie, who is the only remaining family member. Benjamin is a student at Northwest University in Kirkland, Washington, USA. Because of the testimonies he has spread through his social sphere in America, several of his mainly white American friends are now seeking to come to Uganda with the sole purpose to be mothered by Sarah.

According to Sarah, Robert does not have the kind of money that many imagine. The difference with him is that he does not hesitate to share whatever he has with the army of disadvantaged people who dominate his social circles. His ability to mobilize resources and take care of these people creates the impression that he has bottomless pockets with wads of cash stashed away. No matter how much or how little he has, he will give most of it away. However, what is not in dispute, as Sarah says, is the fact that God has blessed her husband with kind people and favored him before many.

Sarah has played a pivotal role in shaping the Queen of Katwe herself, Phiona. When she joined them at their little house, Phiona arrived with the ghetto mentality that lacked the basic etiquette of urban life. She is witness to the gradual changes that Phiona has undergone; from the unwashed slum kid to a responsible girl with a dream. Sarah's close surveillance combined with the disciplinarian nature common to most teachers ensured that Phiona grew into the person Sarah and Robert knew she could be.

Sarah has been particularly keen on helping Phiona and many other girls in the SOM Chess Academy to stay humble and avoid the temptation of getting carried away by the fame that her name is generating across the globe. Thus far, Phiona has been able to contain herself and remain focused on her goal, a key ingredient in the life of Robert Katende. Sarah has also been able to instill some spiritual qualities in her, continually reminding Phiona that she has to stay connected to God and always recognize that without Him, she would never have dreamed of being where she is today. Now, Phiona is looked up to by her peers in Uganda and the U.S. as a role model, not to mention the world over. She is an example to those who aspire to dream big.

This kind of treatment and focus is not limited to Phiona; Sarah has been in the habit of gathering the older girls of the SOM Chess Academy to teach them about the deeper realities of life, such as social ethics in a wicked and fallen world. Most of the girls live with single mothers or have no parents at all, while those who have both parents have suffered all manner of issues, including domestic violence, sexual abuse and the generally lousy influence of growing up in a ghetto. These kids usually have far greater challenges to surmount compared to their urban peers. In recognition of these challenges, Sarah has stood in the gap to offer them what they are unable to find anywhere else—invaluable advice. For all his good intentions and abilities, Robert certainly has limitations on dealing with girls, and that which he cannot do, Sarah has aptly stepped up to the plate. It is a testament to the winning partnership that the couple has made—a classic case of perfectly fitting pieces of the jigsaw puzzle.

It is because of such examples as these above that the notion of "impossible" has been debunked. The axis of Robert, Sarah and Phiona is living proof that indeed nothing is impossible. They show us that impossible is not a fact; it's merely an opinion. Sarah's wish is that their children will bury them with joy and celebration, sending them off because they have run a good race.

Julius Ssali

Contrary to popular belief, Katwe is not the only place where chess was happening as Coach Robert Katende started his journey with chess. In 2004, Coach Robert had his eyes on other places, too, as he sought to balance the needs of different communities around the Kampala metropolis. One of the areas that pioneered this journey is Nateete. Unlike Katwe, Nateete is not known for sprawling slums, although in 2004 it was just an average Ugandan outlying roadside town with small business going on. It lies on the main highway that links Kampala to the greater western and southern regions of Uganda and is typified by endless traffic jams of trucks, buses, commuter taxis, small cars, motorbikes and hordes of people. In the midst of this chaos was a football field adjacent to Nateete police station. It was surrounded by a swampy trench that usually deluged it with flood water whenever it rained heavily.

This is precisely where Coach Robert chose to set up camp. He convinced a group of young people who spent their time watching others playing football and looking for scrap to sell in order to survive to try out the game of chess. Out of the large gang, only six kids agreed to take part, and one of them was Julius Ssali. Just two months after starting the training, Coach Robert singled out Julius to begin training with the other kids in Katwe.

The group sat by the trenches of the pitch playing the board game that was introduced by Coach Robert. They were usually sitting under the hot sun because there was no shelter. Predictably, the group became smaller with time, and after just one year, only one kid was left... and it was Julius. "It was quite understandable and expected," says Ssali. "Chess was a new game and a bit difficult to appreciate, but I already had a strong love for draft, and I liked doing things that involved some calculations." To Julius, the chess and draft boards were very similar, so learning chess seemed like a natural step for him.

Following the dropping out of the rest of the group, Coach Robert decided to permanently add Julius Ssali to the pioneer group in Katwe. Due to the long distance between the two places, Julius was provided transport every Saturday to join the rest of the kids and train for upcoming tournaments. At that time, he was staying with his parents and attending Crane High School in Nateete in Senior 1. The other colleagues at Katwe were Richard Tugume, Brian, Ivan, Samuel and Gerald. It did not take long before Coach Robert began to expose the pioneer team to chess tournaments throughout the country. The first major appearance was a national chess tournament in which they featured as a "special group" because they were young and not from an organized institution (they were competing against high schools). This was more of a confidence-building exercise for them than it was a competition, and it did well in prepping them for the greater challenges up ahead. After three years of testing the ground, they became a force to be reckoned with, as has been told through this book.

Ssali attributes whatever he has achieved in his life thus far to chess. Because of the game, he was able to escape the Nateete ghetto and become more informed and connected to the inner city and to people who matter, as well as seizing many opportunities that he had never anticipated. Chess has taken him to many countries around the world, including Kenya, the U.S. and the Netherlands. He has also won several accolades, including eight medals and two trophies. Currently, Ssali manages the Differently Abled Program based in Gulu, Northern Uganda. This program started in 2016 when Coach Robert and the FIDE (World Chess Body) Vice President came up with the idea to start a chess program for the physically handicapped children in East Africa. This was launched on March 13, 2016 at Kampala School for the Physically Handicapped. Coach Robert started training them in the game of chess for the first two months, then handed the leadership role to Ssali as one of the many instructors he has mentored. At the time of the writing of this book, Ssali has overseen the program for two years.

One of his greatest achievements was when the children represented their school in the National Schools chess tournament in 2017 and came in as second runners-up. Additionally, two of the kids represented the country at the World Youth Chess Championship for the Disabled in the U.S. for two years in a row (2017 and 2018). They were also the only representatives from the whole of Africa.

Richard Buyinza

Richard Buyinza was on the verge of giving up the prospect of ever making it through school, as was the fate of many of his ilk. Richard is the youngest in Phiona Mutesi's family. He was the last among them to join the SOM Chess Academy, after being urged on by Phiona. On the very first day, he found the board game tremendously boring and resolved not to waste his time on it—funny thing was, he had nothing much to do at that time in the first place! He was only eight years old. At that age, he had only just completed his nursery school and had sat out four years without school due to lack of tuition. He continued to intermittently attend the

Chess Academy, albeit mainly to partake of the free porridge meal or else risk starving back at home. That is when Coach Robert picked him up and enrolled him in Universal Junior Primary School located in Katwe, where he joined Primary 1 at the age of eleven—over four years older than the average age for that class. That means he was by far the oldest pupil, and likely would be for the rest of his education.

Shortly after, Richard began to take chess more seriously but was still reasonably uninterested. He consequently began to compete under the children's category in the Father Grimes Tournament. One of the most maddening moments of his young chess career was when he put up a lousy show during a tournament. He won one game and made one draw out of the thirteen games he played. His colleagues who had performed well labeled him the chief food eater at SOM Chess Academy. One of his sole purposes in the academy was to enjoy the maize porridge, but with no real interest in chess, thus the poor performance. This kind of maligning from his colleagues must have stung Richard so hard that he determined to prove to all and sundry that he was not what they thought.

The following term, he took part in the national junior chess championships and scooped up the second position. In third term, he participated in the prestigious Rwanbushenyi chess tournament in the Under-16 category, and he was among the runners-up, from which he won a chessboard prize. From that time forward, he has cemented his place permanently among the top players, and successfully dispelled the earlier insinuation by his friends that he was only good at eating food.

The school that Richard attended sadly collapsed while he was still in Primary 3, which prompted Coach Robert to take him to join St. Mbuga Primary School. The tuition at St. Mbuga was more expensive but the school had a better standard when it came to academics. Robert strategized to pay for private classes to help Richard catch up quickly with the rest in his class. In an unusual run of events, Richard performed so well that because of his age, he was allowed to skip Primary 4 and head straight to Primary 5, owing to his exceptional brilliance in academics. He again excelled at Primary 5, skipped 6 and was placed in Primary 7, defying the odds that had been placed on him previously. Due to his "advanced" age for his level, he was able to leapfrog and mitigate the deficit by two years—an excellent achievement for him at such a time when he was the laughingstock of the younger kids in his class. The fact that he is a tall boy by his natural build did not help matters.

Coach Robert paid for his special private classes. These extra classes, along with his hard work, enabled him to become the second-best student in his school in the Primary Leaving Examinations (PLE), scoring seven aggregates. This was no small feat, considering he had skipped two classes prior to this. Since joining Senior 1, Richard has assumed the top position in his class, virtually every trimester. In 2016, he sat for his Uganda Certificate of Education (UCE) exams and got a first grade. At the time of the writing of this book, he is in an institution pursuing a science course in technical laboratory work. There is a strong indication that Richard is headed for a bright future; nothing could possibly undercut his prospects at making it to the top echelons of career excellence, should he continue this trajectory uninterrupted.

This is the very boy who was nearly lost to the ways of the Katwe slum with no prospect of ever making it through school; this was the brain that was almost relegated to failure. Coach Robert was spot on when it came to seeing his potential, just like he was regarding the boy's elder sister, Phiona Mutesi. This is yet another gift inherent in Robert: his penchant for spotting potential among the most unlikely of people and harnessing it for greater good.

Richard's exploits on the chessboard cannot go unnoticed; he has maintained a consistent streak in winning tournaments ever since that time during his formative years when he was only seeking to save his face. From the time he joined St. Mbuga S.S, he has played Board 1 and claims to have lost count of the gold medals he has won in the process. He has six trophies under his belt so far. He has represented SOM Chess Academy in the national league, had a short stint with the Mulago Rooks Chess Club until 2015, where he played Board 3 and won several medals. In 2016, he played for Comrades Chess Club on Board 3 in the national league.

Richard attributes all his fortunes to Coach Robert, who discovered him in the year 2010 when he had no hope. Since he never got the chance to see his biological father, he looks up to Robert as his father, scarcely any less than how others relate with their real dads. He says that Coach Robert is training him to be a leader and a problem solver. He is strongly driven by the events of the past, which are far from lost on him. When he recalls the domestic challenges he endured as an infant—going without food for days, his mother's struggles to subsist with rent in arrears for months and sleeping in makeshift shacks for years on end—his determination to succeed is a do-or-die affair.

Coach Robert would occasionally remind all the kids in the SOM Chess Academy that their welfare hinged on their excellent performance; if they wanted to continue with their education, eat good food and have rent cleared, then they had to show cause. They had to give their best in everything they did, be it playing chess games or committing to education. Whereas Robert could have used this to boost the kids' morale, they likely took it literally and worked towards out-maneuvering one another in a bid to catch the favorable eye of their coach. This fighting spirit is evident in Richard from the manner in which he speaks and carries himself. There is no second-guessing that he is a man on a mission. This, too, is characteristic of most of the SOM Chess Academy kids.

One of the elements to which Richard attributes his growth is the fact that Coach Robert used his real-life stories while teaching or training them. For instance, Coach would tell them how he grew up without his father and the implications for his life, which are well-articulated in the first part of the book. Like Robert, Richard never got the chance to see his father. He carried with him the conviction that if Coach could make it through life to the point where he was then there was hope for everyone, regardless of their social background. There were also the fellow Chess Academy kids who shared similar stories—orphans, abandoned and denied right at birth by their dads—all hanging on the hope provided by Coach Robert that all was not lost; that they were overcomers in a world set up for them to conquer. This is why the success of Robert's ministry was never about the meager resources, or whether he was able to provide them food; it first and foremost had to do with his influence upon their lives. The transformation of the kids' mindsets from viewing themselves as useless pawns to people with the potential to in turn wield influence on others is the single most important achievement at the academy.

Chess has helped Richard with soft skills that are handy for him to effectively live his life. For example, he has learned a great deal about how to manage his time, borrowing from the idea of using a clock for timing while playing chess. In the same vein, he knows how to budget his time while doing classwork and other related tasks. He has also learned to calculate his moves and become intentional in the decisions he makes, understanding the consequences that may arise. He believes that he will achieve a title in chess someday and harbors plans to attend the World Chess Olympiad in his lifetime.

"Few will have the greatness to bend history itself, but each of us can work to change a small portion of events. It is from numberless diverse acts of courage and belief that human history is shaped. Each time a man stands up for an ideal, or acts to improve the lot of others, or strikes out against injustice, he sends forth a tiny ripple of hope, and crossing each other from a million different centers of energy and daring those ripples build a current which can sweep down the mightiest walls of oppression and resistance."

– Robert F. Kennedy

CHAPTER TWELVE
INSPIRED TO INFLUENCE

THEY SAY THAT you can always spot a chess player from among players of other sports. They will be the ones who will be better prepared to deal with the world, more intelligent and have more knowledge not just about the game, but also about most other things in general. Benjamin Franklin famously said that "The game of chess is not merely an idle amusement; several very valuable qualities of the mind are to be acquired and strengthened by it, so as to become habits ready on all occasions; for life is a kind of chess." This way of thinking is bearing fruit among several of the beneficiaries of the SOM Chess Academy.

Esther Tushemereirwe

Esther Tushemereirwe joined St. Mbuga S.S. in 2009 and quickly became part of the Chess Academy in the school. Her friends advised her that if she wanted to excel in the game, then she had to join the SOM Chess Academy in Katwe during the holidays to train. She was already taking part in several chess competitions, notably the Father Grimes Chess Tournament, and she was the 2012 gold medal winner and silver medalist in 2010 in the same competition. At SOM she met Coach Robert, who immediately took note of her passion and prowess in caring for others. She became a member of the SOM Chess Academy, and Coach Robert was helping to provide some school requirements as her parents struggled to pay the tuition. By the time she joined Senior 6, her parents could no longer afford to keep her in school. Coach Robert requested to meet with her parents to discuss possibilities for her Senior 6 completion. Unfortunately for her, her parents could not find tuition for her Senior 6 candidate class.

Being a girl living in a ghetto, with the level of vulnerability for teenage girls in the slums, Robert promptly enlisted her on the education grant from Sports Outreach, and she was able to complete her Senior 6, going on to later enroll in Kampala University. At the time of the writing of this book, she has completed her degree in procurement and is working with the Red Cross Society at Mengo Hospital in Kampala. Taking a cue from her mentor, she started a chess club at Kampala University, the first one of its kind there, of which she was the captain. The club now has over thirty members! The university now gives bursaries through chess because of her advocacy, leadership and care for others. She plans to stay on as coach for the university after her graduation.

The prospect of furthering Coach Robert's vision is very central in the training of the youngsters at SOM Chess Academy. That the likes of Esther can start up chess clubs at university campuses and even secure bursaries for colleagues is quite telling of a legacy in the making for the mentor. Esther also testifies that playing chess has helped her to expand her thinking capacity as well as learn how to strategize. She offers that most young people have difficulty making critical decisions at their age because their minds are clouded by poor judgment. Thus, they end up falling into temptation and making mistakes just because they don't think critically about the consequences of their decisions. She says that most of her female colleagues at campus tend to focus on the present, consequently giving in to the pressures and pleasures of life. But she has learned to look ahead by calculating the risks of every option, and many times this has helped her to forego certain pleasures for the sake of the better opportunities that the future holds.

Phiona Mutesi

It is quite hard to talk about influence regarding the story of Katwe without reference to Phiona Mutesi. There has been a radical shift in the story of the post-movie Mutesi in more ways than one. *The Queen of Katwe* did a fine job putting her tragedy on the screen and book and shared up to the point where she had fully emerged from the mire and stayed with Coach Robert for a few years. The seed of influence that Robert sowed in Phiona is fast germinating and beginning to bear much fruit. She now ventures out on her own in the U.S.

In August of 2017, Robert started helping Phiona and Benjamin pursue their college education by following a tuition scholarship from Northwest University in Washington. This also became a blessing in disguise because Robert had to figure out how to pay for the board and meals for both, estimated at

$35,000 per year. Robert reached out to Sports Outreach for help, but their grant wouldn't be extended to this cause. He had to determine other ways to raise the funds by himself in order not to miss out on the golden opportunity of the Katwe kids getting into a U.S. college.

The movie had just been released, so there was nothing to expect as a profit percentage as per the understanding with Disney. Robert was determined to find a way to take advantage of the opportunity for his Katwe children to attend a North American university. This gave birth to *The Robert Katende Initiative*, a registered nonprofit organization in the USA. He used this organization to conduct funding through GoFundMe, asking people to donate towards these students' education. The GoFundMe campaign setup was made possible through the support of Robert's friends Karl Reese and Elliott Neff.

The first support given to the Initiative was a one-time donation from International Monetary Fund (IMF). Christine Lagarde, the Director of IMF, had visited Uganda just a year before. On her itinerary, she requested to meet Phiona and Robert while she was there. This meeting led to both Phiona and Robert being invited to speak at the IMF and World Bank Summit in Washington, D.C., where Robert was handed a donation certificate of $10,000 that was later wired to the initiative's account.

The crowdfunding did pretty well. So well, in fact, that Phiona and Benjamin both were able to be enrolled in college. A lot has happened since that time, and to make sense of the new reality that Phiona lives in today, we need to make sense of the events following her relocation to the States. We needed to pick her brain on what really transpired in the heat of the moment, and the kind of bearing that the hullabaloo about the book and movie had on her back in Uganda.

In her own words, she says:

"When they broke the news to me that a movie was being planned about me, none of it made sense at that time. I was in high school then; I was staying with Coach Robert's family. Why would anyone dedicate a whole publication about my life given what I was going through? I didn't know it would be a big deal to the world. But it turned out to be. Even the book promotion that saw me travel to the USA for the first time was still difficult for me to understand. I was told about Disney and their plans to line up a cast that included stars like David Oyelowo and Lupita N'yongo. I had never heard of these names in my life! Even as the movie was being shot in Katwe, I was busy at school pursuing my studies. I went on set a few times; not more than three. I knew little about what actually was going on there because I had books to read and focus on. That was me then.

"That changed, however, when it came to the premiere of the movie. That's when it dawned on me that all along, these people were meaning business. I had never seen anything like that in my life; the kind of media attention that I and the team from Uganda were getting, including Coach Robert and his family, was quite something. We received red carpet welcomes, hundreds of cameras flashing during the World Premiere at the Toronto International Film Festival and media houses making reviews. It's like everyone seemed interested in hearing my story. We sat in the room for the whole day with Coach and interviewers would come in, one by one. We did over forty TV interviews in one day. I was invited to important meetings in America as a guest speaker, even when I couldn't express myself properly in English and had to depend on Coach Robert to interpret some difficult portions. I signed autographs on books and movie copies—all very strange things in my world. The reality was that my life had taken a new turn. Yeah, things changed quite a lot…"

When the world opened up for Phiona, many things that were once distant dreams have since come to pass. For instance, she had heard a great deal about Garry Kasparov, one of the greatest chess players of all time and a Grandmaster from Russia. Phiona had the rare opportunity of a lifetime to play an exhibition game with the former world champion during one of her scheduled visits to the USA. Although the match may have been choreographed and thus ended in a draw, playing on the same board with Gary must have awakened another side of Phiona that she likely did not know. This could have been the final crowning on her head of the honor of the queen that she had previously been christened in books and articles. This, too, must have had a positive bearing on how she would carry herself going forward and how she wished to use this newfound clout as a tool of influence.

The publicity caused more awareness and got us several good friends. It is then that Phiona and Benjamin, through the new friends (and of course, God's favor) got an opportunity to study at the Northwest University, an accredited, Christian institution located in Kirkland, Washington. The fact that she had already made several visits to the USA on various speaking engagements, settling in at Northwest was not that tough of a call. The offer was made on Benjamin's first trip to the USA, when Coach Robert had made arrangements with Elliot and Karl's family for Benjamin to stay there for six months to work on his chess. This time helped Benjamin to get more acquainted with the area.

In order to meet the requirements for the college enrollment, Coach made arrangements for Phiona to take her SAT exams from the USA on that same trip, prior to returning to Uganda. Even Benjamin was registered to do his SAT exams in the period of six months he was with Karl's family. This sounds easy in writing, but it placed a heavy workload on Robert, and he spent sleepless months working and strategizing on how to get money for meals, boarding, and other requirements on top of the tuition that had been offered. It was so stressful that Robert developed regular headaches. He consulted with several doctors and did many scans including an MRI through the support of his friends like Dr. Pomeranz Steven, owner of Proscan in Cincinnati, Ohio. Dr. Steven's family was very supportive of Robert's work, and they made the first donation of $5,000 towards the acquisition of the Katwe Chess Academy Property. This was also matched by a donation from Karl Reese's family. Robert's headaches persisted, and he had to simply endure them amidst all that he juggled, including a master's degree course in International Community Development from Northwest University, for which he had received a scholarship to pursue. Although most of the course was online, it required him to go to Oxford University in London for a week's orientation.

Even in the midst of all the chaos, Phiona and Benjamin eventually got enrolled at Northwest University, which was a huge accomplishment for everyone involved. Who would have thought this would happen—especially after Robert and his wife, Sarah, decided to take on these children to stay with them at their humble abode. After having settled in at the college, predictably, they sought to keep in step with their chess culture. Unfortunately, there was no chess club in place. They approached the president and shared their idea of starting a chess club at the college, to which they received a resounding "yes!"

The president was very excited about the development and pledged to render them whatever support they needed to make it work. He demonstrated this by granting them unfettered access to his office in the event of any need concerning the board game. In a matter of days, the duo had started a chess club, where Phiona holds the role of president and is deputized by Benjamin. Within a month, the club had already attracted over thirty members of the students' community as well as the academic staff. They wasted no time in organizing trainings during the week in preparation for possible tournaments.

In December 2017, less than four months after setting up the club, the first opportunity presented itself in the form of the Pan-America School Competition. According to a Northwest University blog post, the attention moved to center stage when the university chess team won the trophy for the small college team category in its first season of competition. Northwest University clinched the trophy after a sweeping 4-0 victory over defending Champions Oberlin College, which had dominated and taken the trophy in the previous four consecutive years. The Northwest team faced stiff competition en route to victory against chess teams from

Columbia University, Arizona State University, Tecnológico Nacional de México, University of Maryland-Baltimore County, Oberlin College, and University of Minnesota-Twin Cities. At the center of this unprecedented feat for Northwest was the Queen of Katwe, Phiona Mutesi, who played on Board Two, winning three matches and drawing in the other. Her Katwe compatriot, Benjamin Mukumbya, earned three wins on Board One. Teammates Andrew Uptain (first-year transfer) and freshman Walter Borbridge also contributed wins to the team's success.

It is noteworthy to recall that owing to her constant mobility and commitments, Phiona had not participated in any tournaments the whole of 2017. And yet, on her first attempt, she was able to produce a scintillating performance that broke the status quo and winning streak of Oberlin. If a supposedly rusty Phiona could pull that off, one can only imagine what lies in store for her when she eventually returns to her element. She speaks proudly of how the president of her college was excited about their win and the way it put them on the map. Such visibility generated by the Queen of Katwe for a university of such status was not to be taken lightly. At the time of the writing of this book, there were several upcoming competitions in the offing that would continue to write the story of this amazing lady.

It is very probable that despite his belief in Phiona's potential for greatness, such news must be eliciting awe not just from her audiences, but also from Robert Katende himself. Robert is both the life and chess coach of Phiona, two major components that make up the Queen of Katwe. She now not only occupies a position of influence but also has grown her own wings. She can fly without fear of crashing into the social cares and burdens that once dogged her daily life. She embodies the qualities of the man who spent more than a decade molding and shaping her into a woman of meaning: hard work, ambition, imagination, creativity and most importantly, humility.

During the time that Phiona has been playing chess, she has come to perceive it as so much more than just an ordinary board game. To her, chess is a whole universe of life values and invaluable lessons. She attests that there are many things she has learned on her own through her exploits on the chessboard that are helping her in real life. For example, she says chess taught her how to focus on a task. She also learned the habit of perseverance; she never gives up on something that she desires, the same way in which she has to continue playing more chess games regardless of the number of losses she encounters. To the people who think that she is simply a lucky girl who somehow mastered the board game, she reminds them that she lost hundreds of games during her seminal years and even during major international tournaments, and Coach has taught her not to entertain the idea of giving up or thinking that she was inadequate. Coach used to tell them that on the journey of learning, you don't resign until it is checkmate. So, it is in life: never give up. Always hang in there; it's not over until it's over. That's how she came to delete the phrase "give up" from her life dictionary.

Today, Phiona's compatriots are still eking out a living at SOM Chess Academy in Katwe. They look at her and Benjamin as the crown jewels of their academy. The duo is not only the quintessence of success, but also a living example that it is possible to rise from grass to glory. They no longer have to read about the rags to riches stories in books about success; they are living in its midst. The academy children are a living hope that there is a chance for everyone, and all who get to learn about their life journey are inspired to strive for a higher goal with the full confidence that they too will make it, one way or another.

Conversely, Phiona seems hesitant to paint a rosy picture of her supposed fortunes. She understands that her friends (and Ugandans in general) are happy when they get the rare chance to travel, particularly to America: the so-called land of opportunity where dreams come true. However, she is quick to say that a lot of this hullaballoo is out of ignorance because the people who harbor such a mentality are oblivious to the flipside of pursuing the American dream. For instance, when she is at school in the USA, she misses her favorite foods back home, her friends, and more importantly, the beautiful warm weather of Uganda. She believes no amount of opulence can make up for these precious ingredients of life, and for that reason, contrary to popular belief, she looks forward to returning home every summer holiday, and eventually, soon after her course comes to an end.

Usually, those who get the chance to travel to the so-called modern-day Promised Land will give whatever excuse they can find to stay there longer, and many times, remain there for good. That seems to be the last thing on Phiona's mind at the moment. She feels heavily indebted to Uganda, especially to the people who sacrificed everything to ensure she achieves whatever she puts her mind to. Her dream, thus, remains to return home and "pay it back" with service and use of her skills to those in most need.

Concerning Coach Robert, Phiona simply runs short of words to describe the man who has spared nothing to see her scale the heights in chess and life. She recalls how her mum was very skeptical about him during the first days of her encounter with Robert. It was difficult for her to entrust her young daughter into the hands of a total stranger, who was enticing her to join a board game academy that she was clueless about. That coincided with the time Phiona's family was living on the streets, having been thrown out of their ramshackle house after defaulting on rent. Phiona opened up to Robert about their domestic challenges during one of her routine training sessions. Robert was so moved by what he heard that he immediately mobilized funds to rent them a house in Masajja, near Kampala city and away from the Katwe slum. After getting married to Sarah, the young couple took Phiona in to stay with them. Robert did this because it was becoming increasingly unsafe for her to stay at their new home since her mother was never home; she was busy running her petty business from the wee hours of the morning until late at night.

Phiona relates to Robert more as a father than a coach, and is quick to clarify that contrary to popular belief, and despite his contributions, Robert rarely coached her chess. Instead, she learned the game mainly through practice. She says there is nothing she could ever give back to Robert for all that he has done, but only wishes that his dream of further building the SOM Chess Academy comes true.

"The question for each man to settle is not
what he would do if he had the means,
time, influence and education advantages;
but what he will do with the things he has."

                    – Hamilton Mabie

CHAPTER THIRTEEN
MORE THAN JUST A FREE MEAL

Benjamin Mukumbya

FOR THE MILESTONES that he has hitherto realized, it is not farfetched to say that Benjamin Mukumbya, popularly referred to among his Katwe circles as Benja, is a luminary of the chess of Katwe. Benja joined ranks with Phiona Mutesi right from the time they were young and helpless. For Benja, there was the added disadvantage of being orphaned, as his mother walked out on them at their most critical hour; whose fate they still don't know to date and may never know. He was taken on by Coach Robert and his wife Sarah in their new marital home, sharing the living room with Phiona and Gloria.

Benja is inspired by Coach Robert's philosophy about chess: all the pieces start as equal, but how you move them will determine what they eventually become. This means if you are working diligently and doing the things that you ought to do, you will ultimately become that which you want to be. This notion has instilled a rare discipline in Benja that he believes he would never have been able to find without the aid of the chessboard. He belongs to the second generation of chess players of Katwe, tutored by the pioneering group, particularly by Ivan Mutesasira. He joined the SOM Chess Academy by default, as he simply needed to have access to food. He was coerced by his mother, who knew he did not like the game. He has since spent more time with the chess family than with his biological one.

When he started playing chess, he registered rapid progress. So much so that he was selected to be part of the young team that featured at the African junior chess tournament in Sudan, alongside Ivan and Phiona. He made winning the board game at all manner of competitions look as easy as breathing, with countless medals and trophies lining his cabin at home. Noticing his potential, Coach Robert took him to the USA to spend some time with seasoned American chess coach Elliot Neff of Chess4life. The idea was to help him garner sufficient skills to enable him to take a shot at the Olympiad, just like Phiona had. The Reese family agreed to host him.

This trip more than paid off when he was seconded for a scholarship following shortly after Phiona had secured her own at the same college. Coach Robert believes it was the case of being in the right place at the right time and meeting the right people. When the admissions board, led by Dr. Joseph Castlebery, the president of the college, met Robert and Phiona, Benjamin was with them as well and they asked what plans Benja had. They discovered that Benja was awaiting entry into college, and the president personally made the offer for a scholarship right on the spot. This presented a new opportunity for him and Phiona to take their game to a new level—a real test of their mettle.

As has already been told in the section on Phiona above, it has already been a phenomenal run of success for the duo in a short period of time. Benja alludes that initially they started the Chess Academy at Northwest for fun, never harboring any serious desires for competition. They sought to create a new family of chess away from the one they missed so dearly thousands of miles away in Katwe. Little did they know what awaited them! Indeed, the university chess club is fast becoming a true family whereby members of different races share their stories and enjoy each other's company. In a place where nearly everything has a price tag, chess is a source of free fun for Benja and Phiona.

During the 2017 Inter-Collegiate Chess Championships in Ohio, Benja was able to win three of his six games, significantly contributing to the team's overall performance. He played many masters during the tournament and put up a formidable challenge for them. The team won the tournament and received a trophy for Small Colleges Division overall winners. This phenomenal start to their fledgling club generated immense visibility for them, as well as making chess the most active club in the college. As a result, the administration has now thrown its full weight behind it.

Benja is pursuing a Bachelor of Science degree in Biology and plans to become a neurosurgeon someday. Like Phiona, he is unambiguous about his future plans; he wishes to return to Uganda and help out his community using his newly acquired professional skills. He firmly believes that the purpose of his success transcends his ambition and happiness. He is well aware of the weight of the demand on his shoulders, and thus he works towards managing his and others' expectations. His old buddies in Katwe—the ones who taught him chess and those he has played with over the years—all look up to him as their ambassador and have incredibly high hopes in him. Though the chance to be a representative for his people is a high honor, it also comes with great cost, as a let down on his part certainly has a massive bearing on all these people and can even be construed as a betrayal to all.

Moreover, there are more than sufficient incentives for him to compromise his integrity. This is owing to the rather weaker spiritual values in his current environment. Some of his American friends at college have told him that he needn't know some of the things they do because it won't benefit him an inch. This means his colleagues recognize that he still ascribes to his conservative Christian values and thus seek not to "contaminate" him (in their words). There are several Christian fellowships at the campus that he attends, but he has noticed that in nearly all of them, members consciously avoid discussing controversial issues such as terrorism, homosexuality and others. He also has to deal with some mild racist insinuations every so often.

One time, he was instructing a white female student at campus in chess when she commented that she couldn't believe that Benja, a black guy, was teaching her the board game. Even so, he is glad that he and Phiona lead the Chess Academy at Northwest. He sees it as a testimony and proof that God can use anybody—that He is no respecter of persons, as the scriptures say. God can bless and gift anyone as He pleases, regardless of age, race, size, social standing and so forth. This is why, despite their backgrounds of extreme misery and social stigma of their childhood, those who have grown up in the life of privilege have to humble themselves and be taught by Benja and Phiona.

On the other hand, some American folks have frequently mistaken them for rich kids. This is likely because the book and movie that they inspired came from Disney, and Disney is a big money brand. They assume that they must have been paid a significant amount for their role in *The Queen of Katwe*.

Benja reasons that while he and Phiona may be trailblazers in the Katwe world, in terms of exploring the opportunities in the West, there is a lot that awaits the younger generation coming after them. This thinking is based on the notion that during his formative years, SOM Chess Academy was not at the level where it is today. The facilities were very basic, and the resource purse was much smaller. Today, it has its own home, and the learning environment is different. For instance, there are now several young coaches and mentors from the pioneer crop available at the academy to tutor the youngsters, and Coach Robert no longer has to struggle alone. They now boast of more than five hundred chessboards, and the kids no longer have to endure with a bowl of porridge as he did in the initial years; there is now a proper meal of solid food prepared for them. SOM Chess Academy has also established more regional centers in partnership with other development organizations. More importantly, there is enough inspiration for them to act and stay more focused, at least from the stories of Phiona, himself and all those portrayed in both the book and movie. It is for this reason that he believes there is no longer a limit to what can be achieved by the fraternity of Katwe.

Like several of his colleagues, there is no simple way for Benja to describe the kind of influence that Coach Robert has had on him. "He has laid down his life for so many of us," says Benja. The fact that Coach Robert gave up his civil engineering career for Sports Outreach Ministry has never been lost on Benja. He says that Robert continued to make sacrifices as a lifestyle for the entire time that he has known him. He recalls how Coach has been there for them, responding swiftly to a call when a family member of the SOM kids is not well. He is willing to share his knowledge without reservations.

Most importantly, he is God-fearing. He has imparted many positive values to them, most notably for Benja, hard work. Benja knows that many Ugandan youths have a negative attitude towards work. He shared how, despite the load of course work he has to handle, he is still able to connect with people, run the Chess Academy at Northwest and take part in chess tournaments, among other things. No doubt this is all the result of the kind of training that he has received from coach Robert.

Wilson Mugwanya

Wilson Mugwanya is a classic example of a ghetto kid from Katwe who weathered the storms of life to become the second creation of his own proactive design. Having started playing chess in 2006, he belongs to the second generation of children who joined SOM Chess Academy immediately after the pioneers. Like many of his peers, he was compelled by his sister to join in order to access food; not so much because of the prospects ahead, but rather the free porridge meal that was guaranteed at each attendance. True to his sister's word, Wilson's first attempt did not disappoint as he indeed tasted some of the best porridge in his life. For a young boy growing up in severe poverty, this was sufficient motivation to count on, and is precisely how he became a permanent attendee at the academy. But there was one big problem; Wilson was eleven years old at the time, and he had never set foot in a classroom! The average age at which kids start school in Uganda is three to four years. At Wilson's age, his peers were studying Primary five or six and preparing to join high school. His story was akin to that of Richard Buyinza, another colleague at SOM Chess Academy and younger brother to Phiona Mutesi.

In a rare demonstration of his raw brilliance, Wilson participated in the SOM Interproject Chess Tournament, having learned chess only a few months earlier. He went ahead to emerge as the overall winner in the beginners' category, in which Phiona Mutesi also belonged (and happened to be among those he triumphed over). It was after this regular attendance and feat that Robert Katende approached his sister and informed her that Wilson would be enrolled at Molly and Paul Primary School in Kampala. Robert sought to have him skip P1 and go straight to P2, but Wilson failed the interview and was forced to start from the bottom with everybody else. This meant that he was the oldest pupil in his class by far.

Worse still, he joined school during the promotional third term, having missed out on two terms. Robert had to put him under an accelerated learning program with a teacher to coach him at an extra fee. Fortunately, he made it to the next class and never looked back. This golden opportunity that allowed him to join the school, albeit much later than others, was so important to him that he was unfazed by the prospect of being the most mature student in his class for the rest of his student life. He quite obviously had to endure some ridicule from the younger kids, usually accompanied by a nickname. Even so, he made it through the academic levels and is now pursuing mechanical engineering at Nakaseke Technical Institute. Wilson has also grown and excelled in chess, with five medals won in the school tournaments and placing second overall in the Interproject chess tournament in 2015.

Playing chess has had a significant impact on Wilson in many ways. He not only improved in his science subjects, particularly mathematics and physics, but also found it easy to choose mechanical engineering over other alternatives as his choice career path. Calculating moves against an opponent in a constrained timeframe has ensured that he learns to think fast and make good use of his intellectual faculties. He plans to become a chess instructor at different levels, as well as an automobile engineer. Currently, he spends most of the time mentoring kids in chess at the SOM Chess Academy in Katwe. He sees that these kids have the makings of a great future because they are shaping their minds at a young age.

The one thing that Wilson believes is Coach Robert's greatest achievement is his ability to get the ghetto out of the heads of the kids under his care. Living in the slum is a big challenge and can greatly influence the way one thinks, but Robert trained Wilson (and so many others) to rise up above the ghetto mentality. Even though Wilson continued to live in the ghetto for years, his attitude changed for the better. Robert led him to Christ during the several engagements whereby they would have Bible study at the end of the trainings, as the coach shared both his life stories and the lessons learned on the chessboard.

Martin Musiime

Martin Musiime is the 2013 Uganda National Junior Chess Champion. He joined the Katwe chess fraternity at a later stage in 2009, while he was a student at St. Mbuga Vocational Secondary School. He was influenced by his friends Tugume Richard and Brian Mugabi, then students in that school. They taught him chess in between classes, and soon after encouraged him to join the SOM Chess Academy, to which he obliged. They continued to train him on the board game until he was properly grounded. While in Senior 3, his parents were overwhelmed by the tuition demands and opted to put him out of school. Thankfully, he was able to join the SOM Scholarship Program through Coach Robert and was able to complete high school. Martin then went on to Mbarara University of Science and Technology in Western Uganda on a government sponsorship, where he attained his Bachelor of Science in Education Degree.

During his earlier years in life, particularly in high school, Martin led an independent life whereby he saw little need to work with others. However, that changed when he encountered chess. He was taught that the pieces on the chessboard must work in concert with each other in order to achieve their shared goal of winning. This prompted him to open up and start working with other people, as this presented better possibilities for accomplishing anything. Through the simple game of chess, he learned things like goal setting, planning and a raft of other life skills. Martin now works as a science teacher in one of the international schools in Uganda. He is making a reasonable amount of money, out of which he helps others who are in dire need of a push to achieve their own dreams. He also wishes to continue with education by pursuing his dream course in civil engineering.

Martin is certainly not short of models in his life to pick a leaf from. He has learned from Phiona Mutesi that with hard work and perseverance, anything is achievable. He has watched Phiona gradually rise from the muck to the position she has now and believes that while some of it may border on the miraculous, there is also a great deal of personal effort she inputted as well.

Coach Robert remains by far his greatest inspiration. He shares that Coach Robert is a very compassionate man who loves to see people develop and advance to their full potential. Because of the manner in which Robert turned around his life, Martin wants to see the same transformation happen with others, and he has made it his life's mission to fulfill it.

Richard Kato

When Gertrude Nanono discovered that there was a secret treasure, both in chess and at the Sports Outreach Ministry in Katwe, following months of misgivings, she decreed that all her children would join the outfit willy nilly. Certainly, her initial expectation was limited to the prospect of a free mug of corn soup daily, which she could not afford to give to her three children. One of the children who heeded their mother's directive was Richard Kato, a twin brother to Stella Babirye. He joined the academy in 2008 at age eight. He was lucky to have done so at the right time, when he was "age appropriate" for his class (P2), unlike some of his colleagues who were much older. He went through the education system and soon joined St. Mbuga Vocational S.S. for his high school, from where he completed his Ordinary Level with a second grade. He then went to pursue a degree in Catering and Hospitality Management at YMCA Kampala.

Richard has actively participated in the competitive chess world of Katwe since joining SOM. However, his accolades in the board game came much later. In 2016, he got the opportunity to play in the National Super 12, where he was selected among the best to represent the country. He finished 9th overall, and although this wasn't his desired position, he made a big statement of intent for future prospects. This came to pass sooner than expected, when in 2017 he emerged as the National Junior Chess Champion, the pinnacle of achievement in the game for his level at the local level. He followed this up closely by clinching third place in the 2017 SOM Interproject Chess Tournament.

With a bright future ahead of him, Richard feels like he is just getting started on his journey into the world of chess. During holidays, he volunteers his time training youngsters at the SOM Chess Academy in Katwe. During some of the chess tournaments, he has been able to tap into a vast social network of people who are much older and quite well connected.

One of the greatest principles he has learned from Coach Robert, which he intends to make the best use of, is that one has to use what he has in order to get what he doesn't have. He has hitherto been actively discovering himself, identifying his core strengths so that he can consciously apply them to get himself around. So far, he is confident that chess and education are some of those things, so he does not take them lightly. He is deeply inspired by the story of Coach Robert; how he was able to use his old chessboard to attract the pioneers to start what has now become a phenomenon in Uganda and around the world. Richard believes that with some dedication and persistence, everyone has something that he or she can use to replicate the good work Coach Robert did for them. His ultimate dream for chess is to become a master someday.

Stella Babirye

Stella Babirye is a daughter to Gertrude Nanono and twin to Richard Kato. Their entire family, and Stella in particular, constitute a significant pillar in the story of *The Queen of Katwe*. Unlike her brother Richard, she joined SOM Katwe much earlier. She joined in 2006, in P2 while she was barely eight years of age. After learning the game rather quickly, she began to rack up some wins. In 2014, she clinched the trophy for the Uganda National Junior Chess Championships and was also declared as the overall winner of the 2017 edition of the SOM Interproject Chess Tournament in the ladies' category. A visit to their humble home (that was realized through Coach Robert's work) reveals their living room teeming with silverware, trophies and medals, all jostling for space on the cement floor. She has previously represented Uganda's Junior Chess team in Angola for the Africa Juniors Chess Championship as well.

Stella had the rare opportunity to be cast in *The Queen of Katwe* movie, in which she had the chance to fly to South Africa where part of the filming was done. It was from part of her wages that their family land was purchased, with the help of Coach Robert. She is continuing with her high school education and harbors plans to become one of the political leaders in her country, and to coach chess as well. Chess has taught her to stay focused, and she is very confident that the storms of life and pressures of growing up as a young girl with a single mother will by no means cause her to go off her chosen course of life. She aspires to become the Speaker of the Parliament of Uganda.

Derrick Mirembe

Derrick is among the most recent crop of members of the SOM Chess Academy, having joined the family in 2014. He attended St. Mbuga Vocational S.S. and learned chess in 2012 under the patronage of his schoolmates from SOM Katwe. They convinced him to take time off and visit the center in Katwe during holidays in case he wanted to excel in his chess skills. He willingly accepted their invitation, having earlier observed that chess players at his school were usually among the best-performing students. He too noticed a tremendous improvement in his own grades from the time he started playing chess. This was a result of the practical lessons picked from the chessboard, such as the virtue of time management, quickness in decision-making and social conduct, and the fact that all actions have consequences. Observance of these virtues had quite a bearing on his focus and performance in his studies. Derrick is an orphan who entirely relied on one of his aunties for survival. Unfortunately, she could not afford his high school education tuition, so he dropped out of school until he was bailed out by Coach Robert and put on the list of children supported through the Chess Academy.

Derrick is now a third-year student of Mechanical and Manufacturing Engineering at Kyambogo University in Kampala. He is also an instructor at SOM Katwe. The opportunity to render his services at SOM Katwe has instilled in him a confidence that he did not have before; the ability to stand before crowds and address them or pass on his skills to them. It has also improved his social networks. Coach Robert always reminds them that their principal object as chess players is not just to win games and trophies, but also learning to make and maintain friendships. Winning a match should simply be seen as a bonus. He has learned to respect others as well as observe rules. If you don't follow the rules of the chess game, then there are higher chances of losing the game. Even more, he has learned to interpret and relate chess to the Bible and real life situations. He has observed and learned excellent leadership skills from Coach Robert, along with so many other life lessons. Derrick speaks of Robert as someone who is prayerful, listens to everyone, and is ready to humble himself to the level of anyone, regardless of social standing.

Dorothy Nassali

Dorothy Nassali was a typical Katwe slum dweller who identified with the likes of Harriet Nakku, Phiona Mutesi's mother. She and her twins, Isaiah Wasswa and Lydia Nakato, lived together with her little brother Wilson Mugwanya in a single room in Nkere, one of the nastiest quarters of Katwe. One time, Coach Robert brought a chessboard to a shop in the immediate neighborhood and encouraged neighborhood kids to start training. However, Nassali objected to the idea as she did not see its worth at that time—especially when her twins, who were four years old at the time and their brother Wilson was six years old, would go without food quite frequently. But when she discovered that kids who attended training were given a free cup of porridge, she not only sent Wilson for the training but also gave him two extra cups to bring some for her twins. In their case, the porridge was a real lifesaver (not to mention divine intervention) as their situation was so dire.

While Nassali was still delighted in the relief of the porridge that was usually served for breakfast, Coach Robert soon introduced lunch as well. This new incentive made Nassali believe all the more that this, without doubt, was the beginning of hope in her otherwise hopeless situation. The family began to feed off the porridge, posho and beans that Robert provided, even though only Wilson attended the chess club. This situation was quite similar to many of the families in the Katwe community.

One time, Wilson returned home from his routine training and told Nassali that Coach Robert had told them to dress up in their best clothes in preparation for a chess tournament that would take place that day. She recalls dressing him up in non-matching slippers and a clean shirt. When he returned from the tournament, he was full of joy as he broke the news to his big sister about beating a "big man" in his chess game. This was his first big victory in chess against an adult, and quite obviously the harbinger of many more victories that would typify his subsequent years. Although she knew nothing about chess, Nassali saw her faith come alive with every new positive story that her little brother brought home. At the time, Wilson was attending a rural school where tuition was a paltry 30,000 shillings (approx. $8) per trimester. He would often report to school late because he first had to hawk charcoal stove lighting sticks around the slum to raise some income.

After two years, Coach Robert asked Nassali for her phone number. She gave him that of her husband, since she didn't own a phone. Robert promptly asked them to send Wilson for interviews at Molly and Paul Primary School. Wilson was offered a vacancy, but in P2 instead of P5.

Seeing the miracles that were taking place in her brother's life, Nassali wasted no time in enrolling the twins in the Katwe chess club while they were attending Katwe Primary School. Meanwhile, Wilson finished P7 with a first grade and went to St. Mbuga Vocational Secondary School on a SOM education scholarship, becoming the first person in Nassali's family to go beyond that level of education. One day, Coach Robert surprised her with a phone call, inquiring about her twins' performance in class. During those days she worked as a waitress in a small restaurant in Nakasero market, located right in the heart of Kampala city. The meager earnings she made went towards house rent and fees. She toiled on her own as her husband contributed nothing to their welfare. She told Robert that the kids were never given reports due to constant fees defaulting. She also informed him that the kids would go to school on empty stomachs daily, as the school did not provide any meals, making it hard for them to perform well.

Their combined school fees were about 150,000 shillings ($40), yet they were in arrears for a full year. Robert did not have the full amount of money, but still managed to raise 24,000 shillings ($7), which he gave her immediately. Overwhelmed by joy, she dashed to school and paid in the money to the head teacher, who was very surprised and handed her the reports. Coach Robert then transferred the twins to Kibuye Junior School, a much better school than the previous one. When they returned from the interviews, they had brand new school uniforms, sportswear and school bags—things they had never possessed since they started schooling. Since she could not afford to buy one, Nassali would dress her little girl Nakato, of hardly ten years of age, in her own skirt as her daily school wear. Coach Robert also started providing regular domestic supplies such as food stuffs and other needs. Life became more manageable for the family as the things that previously dogged their lives were now in the past.

During the production of *The Queen of Katwe* in 2015, Nassali, together with her daughter Nakato, were auditioned as extras in the movie at the recommendation of Coach

Robert. They were both cast in roles for which they were paid. Nakato received slightly more due to her bigger role. This came as a major financial breakthrough for the family! Robert asked Nassali to open an account with Centenary Bank in which her money and that of her daughter Nakato was banked. They now had a combined wage of 1,900,000 shillings ($510).

Nassali had never dreamt of making such an amount of money in her life, so much so that upon confirming the wire transfer, she had to ask several strangers on her way back home from the bank to ascertain the amount indicated on the bank slips. When Robert asked her what she wanted to do with the money, she told him she wanted to acquire a plot of land. He immediately helped her purchase a plot of land in Bujuuko, the same area where Phiona Mutesi built a house for her mother.

Today, Dorothy Nassali lives in her own house that was built with the support of Coach Robert, more than 30km away from the torment of the Katwe ghetto. Her twins, who are now fourteen years old, are fully engaged in chess, in which they are performing very well. Currently, Nakato is under the full care of Coach Robert, who took her to the SOM Chess Academy in Kiwawu, Mityana road, where her education and personal needs are taken care of in full. Sadly, Nassali separated from her husband some six years ago. She is a committed Christian and says she is living the dream of her life.

Sharif Wasswa Mbazira

At eighteen years of age, Wasswa Mbazira was easily the best chess player in the differently abled category in Uganda. He was born with a disability that crippled all four of his limbs, and he could neither use his legs nor his hands normally. Moving pieces on the chessboard require him to have some additional support. He figured out early in life that because of his condition, he would need to put to use his talents in a way that did not demand much physical activity. This is how he started playing draft during his formative years at the Kampala School of the Physically Disabled.

In 2016, while he was in P5, he was introduced to chess by Coach Robert Katende. The first lot was picked among kids who played draft, although Sharif was initially left out. They were told that they would be introduced to a new board game called chess, which none of them had heard of yet. The group started with over 500 members, but soon the numbers fells to a measly ten, and eventually to five kids as others reverted back to their old draft game.

Sahrif has endured a lot of rejection because of his disability. His situation was so severe that he needed support with almost everything, including bathing, feeding and movement. Even his immediate relatives rejected him because his disability was viewed as a burden to them. However, he endures all this rejection with grace, simply because he has no other option. He has been exercised in the virtue of persistence, and eventually, this persistence finally paid off. That same year, he took part in the first tournament organized by Coach Robert, and he emerged as the champion. In the same year, he participated in the school's Junior Chess Tournament, where he was given Board 1. The 2017 Interproject chess tournament was his fourth major appearance on the national scene.

His first international chess appearance was in 2017, when he represented the country in the FIDE Differently Abled Chess Championships that took place in Orlando, Florida, USA. There, he managed to clinch some two points. In August 2018, he once again attended the same tournament that took place in Georgia, USA, where he got two and a half points. In both tournaments, he played with people of diverse nationalities, particularly Arabs and Americans. To qualify for the first international tournament, he had to win the local chess tournament in order to emerge as the Ugandan representative. Since there was no tournament organized at the local level in 2018, he was chosen as the national representative based on the results of the previous year, along with John Mwesigwa, who was the second best in the tournament. Among the countries that took part in the 2018 tournament were USA, Russia, Germany and Uganda. The US took top position, while Uganda placed third. Sharif won a medal and a trophy for Uganda.

Sharif's dream is to earn enough money from chess in order to be able to support himself without the aid of his family. He also dreams of building a bigger house for his family so they can get out of the small one that can barely contain them all. According to Sharif, chess has taught him not only to be more calculative on the board game, but in real life he has learned to plan and weigh his decisions with the view to minimize risk.

"Coach Robert has helped so many people, and I am just one of them," Sharif says. "I hope that myself and all those that have benefitted from him can also help others." He owes much gratitude to Coach Robert for all that he has been able to achieve at his age, without whose support all would remain just that—a dream. For instance, before meeting Coach Robert, the idea of ever traveling to another country, much less the USA had never crossed his mind. Yet, with the help of chess and Coach Robert, he has seen incredible opportunities unfold in his life. In his condition, he had little hope of ever amounting to anything, but now he can clearly see where he is headed, and it looks brighter than ever.

CHAPTER FOURTEEN
THE KING OF KATWE

In January 2018, in concert with the Robert Katende Initiative, SOM Chess Academy organized the annual SOM Interproject Chess Tournament. It was the 13th edition and attracted two hundred and ninety-six participants from Kampala slums centers, mainly in the age brackets of 5-20 years. There were also about forty youths above twenty. In the same year in March, Robert hosted over 120 young people for a similar tournament in the northern Uganda district of Gulu. The Gulu 8th edition was won by Draga Matthew, the only deaf and mute participant in the tournament. In the same year, the 3rd edition for the Nairobi Mukuru slum in Kenya, also took place and two instructors from Katwe, Julius and Brian, traveled to officiate at the Championship that attracted 280 children below sixteen years.

Coach Robert's vision has grown in leaps and bounds from its six committed pioneers in 2004. It is now a massive family spread beyond the precincts of Katwe to Greater Kampala and other regions of the country, Africa and other continents. This, in essence, means Robert's reputation and clout have also grown in proportion to his vision. He has, in effect, become Uganda's foremost kingmaker in the world of chess, raising an army of young men and women who are obsessed with the board game and turning the wheels of fortune for many.

Phiona Mutesi emerged as the Queen of Katwe, having been picked and groomed by Robert, trained both in chess and in the ways of life, taking her all the way to the Olympiad in Russia and to the point of earning recognition in Uganda and around the world. The question anyone who reads Robert's story would have then would be: "What does this then make him?"

Whereas Coach Robert has never been to the Olympiad as a player, save for standing in as the Uganda national team leader and captain on such occasions as the one Phiona Mutesi and company participated in, his accomplishments are not easy to measure. The enormity of strides that he has made point to very bold steps that speak volumes about his silent achievements.

The Queen of Katwe was originally about Phiona Mutesi, and yet, down the road, it became increasingly apparent that Robert Katende was actually the centerfold of not just Phiona's, but all the kids of Katwe's stories. It is said that the makers of the movie thought at some point that perhaps the production should have been a portrayal of Robert Katende's incredible exploits in the sprawling ghetto. There is no better way to capture this notion than to hear from some people of repute who are witness to the work of Robert Katende.

Tim Crothers

Tim Crothers was very instrumental in the construction of the story of the chess world of Katwe. His book *The Queen of Katwe* opened the eyes of the world to the young Phiona Mutesi and many of her ilk; how these "pawns" are able to ride the storm of ghetto life and become people of significance. Tim is very much aware of the personality of Robert, both before and after the publication of his book, and anyone can bet that if he had the chance to write another book about the subject, he would have a whole lot more to say about him. His personal sentiments about Robert in three words are unequivocal: tireless, fearless, compassionate. His impression of Robert Katende insofar as his personality is concerned is that he is a bright light, a beacon that both draws people to him and shows them the way once they have connected. Regarding Robert's role in discovering and creating Phiona Mutesi and other equally compelling characters in Katwe, Tim attests that it is one of the most remarkable journeys in this world. To grow up as Robert did and simply survive is extraordinary, but to then take his life experiences and use them as a model to help thousands of underprivileged people transform their lives as he did is one of the most amazing success stories of our time.

As to whether to refer to a "King" or "Queen" of Katwe, Tim argues that, "There are many reasons why they chose to primarily focus on Phiona in *The Queen of Katwe*, but I have always said that without Robert there would be no Phiona, while without Phiona there would still be a Robert." Tim further states that "I am constantly amazed at Robert's energy and drive. He wakes up every day and does the work of a hundred men, refusing to rest until he's done as much good as possible in one day. I always tell people that Robert is as close to a saint as anybody I have ever met. He has given them hopes and dreams. Anyone who has ever visited Katwe knows that it is a place that does not foster hopes and dreams. Nobody dreams there until they meet Robert and he provides them the hope to create their own dreams as Phiona did." In conclusion, Tim asserts that if he were to write a book or make a film about Robert Katende, he would call it: "King of Katwe" or "The Fixer."

If equating Robert to the King of Katwe seems like an overestimation, here is an outsider who has closely interacted with Robert (and continues to do so), and his deduction about him is scarcely any less than that of a saint. There is a strong inclination, not just by Tim Crothers, but indeed by most people who have encountered Robert's extravagant generosity, to paint him as a larger-than-life creature comparable only to heavenly beings. That cannot be far from the truth.

Susan Khan

Susan Khan, a Canadian national and personal friend of Robert Katende, has a profound impression about the coach as well. Susan says there are so many words to describe Robert, but if she could choose three of them, they would be: loyal, compassionate and determined.

"My first impression of Robert is that he is a courageous man that has great depth to him. He has used and honed his skillset—both acquired and learned along the way—and coupled it with a good dose of humanity to care, nurture, guide and pave the way for those in need. He offers a physical presence where there might be none; a lending hand, a listening ear and a shoulder to lean on. I find Robert to have a good sense of humor balanced with a level of seriousness. Robert most certainly exudes dedication, passion, hard work, generosity and risk-taking characteristics, which I believe have helped him not to succumb to neither external nor internal forces. Most of us can agree that we all face some level of personal barriers along with the many challenges that life can bring. However, Robert has handled these challenges in an exemplary fashion," says Susan.

Concerning Robert's journey in discovering Phiona and company and turning their lives around, she quips thus, "I think it is absolutely phenomenal! It is without a doubt an extraordinary journey that I do not think Robert or any of the pioneers could have dreamed of or imagined the trajectory that their lives have taken from a seemingly simple game like chess. What makes this more extraordinary, however, is that this initiative was founded by a local Ugandan man called Robert Katende. He has been able to see the initiative grow organically as opposed to a foreigner parachuting in, starting up something, only to leave and have it eventually perish. Not having any Ugandan lineage, myself (at least not that I am aware of), I could not be any prouder of Robert, Phiona, Benjamin and all of the pioneers for their tireless work and success. I feel this is both surreal and heaven-sent. It invokes the likeness of a universal connection and how each and every one of us is directly linked to this unlimited web that bonds us together as one, merging and morphing into something much bigger. Robert needed those kids, and those kids needed Robert. I do not believe it was by mere chance, but rather universal intervention. This ultimately stands as a testament of unity and humanity. When we unite towards a common goal, like Robert and the pioneers have shown, the results can be beyond expectation."

Susan believes in the adage "There are two sides to every story." However, this particular story of Coach Robert is multifaceted and continues to unfold. While *The Queen of Katwe* pays homage to Phiona and her incredible achievements, it also does a fantastic job of revealing Robert's story without taking away from the heroine. The main attraction to *The Queen of Katwe* is that it is a story based on the life of a young girl who rises from the slums to become one of the world's best-known chess players. However, Robert's story is the silver lining within the movie, and it is beautifully and powerfully told without him being the focus. This is precisely why she reached out to Robert after seeing it for the first time.

Susan thinks that some of the character traits that contribute to making Robert an outstanding individual are empathy, humility, understanding, faith, and the ability to easily handle adversity and pressures. When she looks at the story and how it unfolds, all of these traits are firmly entrenched. This, to her, is why Robert's story comes through so powerfully—because he has great character. You may equate it to how one may say that someone is from "good stock."

Susan speaks of the people who have gone through Robert's hands and what she imagines they think of him, positive that they have a tremendous amount of gratitude. Those he comes across and engages with go away with a lasting positive impact because of his personal contribution to their lives and livelihoods. They, without a doubt, have a reverence for Robert. They are driven to success not only for themselves, but as a means to compensate for his efforts and impact that he has had on their lives.

"Our history both molds and contributes to who we are," adds Susan Khan. "This is especially so for Robert Katende. He was orphaned at a very young age and struggled through life to get one of life's single most powerful tools: an education. With the odds stacked against him, what an achievement in itself! Robert, I think, knows all too well the realities of life—the spoken and unspoken, particularly the atrocities that children in poverty endure. The trap and unforgiving realities that are part and parcel of poverty. He did not just get himself out and forget about where he came from. I feel that Robert had done a little digging within—be it conscious or unconscious. So, by the time he was surrounded or in proximity to others facing challenges, he had the intuitive sense and ability to recognize and connect.

"While he had come from far, there was still some ways to go... and while he was still grappling with some loose ends, the children he encountered became his focus; his guiding light, banishing his own worries to the periphery. Robert did not internalize his worries and allow them to consume him, but rather he focused on others, which ultimately not only expanded his own world but the world of all those that would be touched by the presence and what became known as SOM.

"So, yes, I believe that Robert's motivation stems from his own childhood, and I believe he knows and recognizes his privilege and is honored to be able to wake up every day knowing that he is giving back, contributing and touching the lives of so many. To support and assist so many children in perhaps the same circumstances as his own childhood. This alone gives him an authority and credibility that the children can respect, relate to and be motivated by."

Susan says that if she had the resources, she would love to invest in the expansion of the SOM Chess Academy program all across Uganda, so that no child is left behind. To sum it up, she says that the most suitable title that she would come up with for Robert (books and movies alike) has been "The Real Godfather." She confesses that she personally has never quite understood the role that God and/or parents really played, though on a past summer day she was thinking and analyzing what Robert does and the immeasurable impact that his work has on so many precious lives. That is when she came up with alternative titles such as: "Porridge & Chess," "Second Coming," or "From Pawn of the Slum to the Master of Chess Life."

David Oyelowo

To Hollywood movie buffs, David Oyelowo is a man who requires no introduction. He is a classically trained stage actor who has quickly become one of Hollywood's most sought-after talents. His highest-profile role to date was as Martin Luther King Jr. in the 2014 biographical drama film *Selma*. He also took the lead role in *A United Kingdom* (2016). He has played supporting roles in the films *Rise of the Planet of the Apes* (2011), *Lincoln* (2012), *Jack Reacher* (2012), and garnered praise for portraying Louis Gaines in *The Butler* (2013). On television, he played MI5 officer Danny Hunter on the British drama series *Spooks* (2002–2004).

David had the opportunity to play Coach Robert Katende in *The Queen of Katwe*. Expressing what it felt like interacting with the real-life coach and what sentiments he invokes, David has quite a lot to say. In three words, he says coach Robert can be described as patient, sacrificial and kind. Robert is an incredibly resilient person, especially considering the difficulties he met as a child and how he was able to look at his life with the attitude that he wouldn't want others to go through the same. "How he turned that hardship into positive energy was truly amazing," David says.

David thinks that Phiona Mutesi and company are aware that their lives could have gone a different way had they not interfaced with Robert at that time. Despite playing coach Robert in the movie, David does not necessarily believe that he (Robert) should have been the central attraction of the film because, from his experience, often film plots don't go for the obvious. In the end, it was Phiona who went ahead to become a chess genius, despite the circumstances that she had to contend with. Phiona is now an inspiration to the future generation. Moreover, Robert does not seem to feel the pressure to exert himself as the "creator" of Phiona and all her compatriots.

"When I spent time with Robert during the shooting of *The Queen of Katwe* in Kampala, I realized that he is someone that makes you want to be a better person, simply because his degree of compassion is amazing," says David. "If there were more people like Robert, the world would be a much better place." David went on to concede that most of the men who have seen the film have confessed how they want to love their children more. He recalls the day a stranger stopped him at the airport to tell him how he made it a habit to watch and celebrate the movie with his grandchildren once every month, just so they can pick some lessons from it and become better people.

David Oyelowo believes that Robert's magnanimity largely stems from his deeply entrenched Christian values and faith, which lend him the redemptive element—following the example of Jesus Christ—of coming from nothing and giving everything. It could be for this reason that David would rather not rate Robert's achievements because he thinks the coach does not need anyone's approval; his work transcends ranking.

Chess was never among the pastime activities for David's family, but after his experiences in the making of the movie, his house is now littered with chessboards, and his children love the board game a great deal. For all his efforts, David believes Robert needs all the material support he can get in order to further his dream. If he had the opportunity to give a title to a movie about Robert, he would call it "Saint Robert."

Thomas Luther

Last but not least, one of the most recognizable figures to express their sentiments about Robert Katende is German chess prodigy and Grandmaster, Thomas Luther. In 2000, Thomas was a member of the German team that won the silver medal in the 34th Chess Olympiad in Istanbul. Luther is a three-time German Champion who reached the Top 100 in the world. He is a highly successful coach, and one of only a handful of people to be awarded the title of FIDE Senior

Trainer. Becoming a Grandmaster is the dream of every young chess talent. Luther achieved this goal despite the added challenge of being born with a physical disability. Luther is the author of a publication entitled "Chess Reformation," in which he provides a wealth of practical tips and suggestions for chess players of all levels. Using the experiences and insights gained from his remarkable career, Luther offers an insider's view into the world of grandmaster chess.

In February 2017, Uganda's team that was selected for the annual Zonal African Chess championships in Ethiopia was privileged to benefit from the Luther's experience courtesy of SOM Chess Academy. Thomas held a three-day workshop at the Pope Paul Memorial Centre in Kampala, Uganda that was also attended by SOM children from Katwe and other slum centers. During this occasion, Thomas also introduced the team to blindfold chess, a form of chess play wherein the players do not see the positions of the pieces or touch them. This forces players to maintain a mental model of the positions of the pieces. Moves are communicated via a recognized chess notation.

Thomas and Robert enjoy a genial relationship that is bonded by their mutual love for chess as well as the desire to impart skills about the board game. During their frequent interactions, Thomas was able to peek into the world of Robert Katende. He describes Robert as a person who is obsessed with the values of leadership, passion and kindness. He asserts that Robert is a natural leader and that his ability to motivate people is most impressive. Thomas' greatest attribute of leadership to Robert is founded on the understanding that although the credit for the chess program in

Katwe belongs to Robert, the best leaders do not seek fame but results—a quality that is inherent in Robert. Thomas also testifies that Robert is the friendliest person he knows.

Concerning Robert's goal of changing lives one move at a time, Thomas is unambiguous about his support. "I consider it a great idea since chess changed my life, too. I feel very sympathetic towards Robert's mission. I have been to Katwe and other places in Uganda for teaching chess and I would go there again any time," he says. Asked what he would name the book or movie about Robert if he had the chance to, he would call it, "The King of Katwe."

*

Becoming great one move at a time poses a big question to us all: Who is the greatest among us? There is no doubt we are all longing to be great at something; some more than others. There is an innate desire in us to be recognized as the greatest. However, as we see through the life of Robert, the ones who achieve the most are often the humblest. He would never brag about his achievements, so we set out to ask the people he has impacted the most to brag about them for him. And that, dear reader, is the mark of a true leader, for ultimate greatness is seen in the words of Jesus, "Anyone who desires to be first shall be last, and the servant of all."

AFTERWORD

As I LOOK back on all the challenges I faced and somehow managed to surmount in the early part of my life, what I come back to again and again is the power of education. When I look at the students who our Chess Academy was able to help through the transformation of their lives, it is clear that education played a significant part. In the aftermath of the success of *Queen of Katwe* and all the attention that it brought the students and the community as a whole, again I come back to the importance of education. The thread that has bound everything together, that has lifted me and a whole generation of young people out of the ghetto and into the world at large, is education.

When I was given the chance to pursue education, I flourished. In the times when I could not afford it, and the privilege was taken away from me, or even when the *risk* of it being taken away from me existed, I struggled immensely. Everything I discovered about any skills or hidden gifts I had came from the experience of being in a school, guided by teachers and surrounded by other curious young people clamoring for the opportunity to learn and grow. We were desperate to grasp on to something; to elevate ourselves out of poverty and into a better place where we could build a future. We were physically hungry, had few or no earthly possessions, and very little to go home to when school was over. But at school, we had possibility—the possibility of the whole world at our fingertips.

When I first set up the SOM Chess Academy, I wanted to give my students that same sense of possibility that I had discovered as a student; the same understanding that through education, they too could find their unique skillsets and hidden gifts. I wanted them to see that their external circumstances did not reflect their internal capabilities. I wanted them to be empowered through whatever knowledge and resources and information we could share with them. I also wanted to feed them—for some of my earliest recruits, the prospect of the free bowl of corn porridge we provided each day was the incentive to sign up. However, once they were fed, I hoped that they would then consider the possibility of what the program had to offer. I hoped they would understand that through learning, and through chess, they could create futures where they someday would have the means to buy their own food for themselves and their families. I hoped that education and all of its promise would be as life-changing for them as it was for me.

With all of this in mind, I am looking forward to the future. My biggest focus right now is to expand the SOM Chess Academy and Robert Katende Initiative, taking them to a whole new level. I have a vision: I want to set up a school. I do believe, currently in the world, that education has been commercialized, especially in developing countries. This disproportionately impacts those who are at a disadvantage financially. It just so happens that the less privileged—who cannot afford the good schools, or in some cases, cannot afford *any* school—always fall behind those who can pay because they do not have access to the same education. Our school will work to address the problem of lack of provision for a quality education.

My vision is to set up an organization that will establish a school that will provide quality education that can compete favorably with private schools that are too expensive for the vast majority of families to afford. Our school will focus on all the traditional tenets of education, but in addition to that, our school will focus on using chess principles and concepts that not only enhance the students' academic performance, but also teach the students soft skills that help them be more articulate in their daily lives. There are all kinds of life lessons that can be learned from chess, as I've talked about a bit in this book. Our school will hinge very much on our chess concepts. This is what we understand is the best way that we can empower our young generation to take up the day-to-day challenges in their respective communities as problem solvers and agents of change. We have already seen many youths who have advanced in terms of what we are trying to teach, thanks to the impact of chess in their lives.

Right now, there is a considerable gap countrywide in Uganda (as well as other countries) that we are lacking in the artisan sector. These are people who have the skills needed for development, and this is what we have already started to address on a smaller scale.

We already have a computer lab with about twelve computers, and we are trying to develop computer skills for the students. My vision is that we can grow this to another level so that we can focus more on coding, graphics and programming. With the pace of technology and technological growth in the world, the need for the development of both life and vocational skills in terms of computing is enormous. My hope is for the children in Uganda to join the ranks of those developing apps, software, programs and graphics, both earning a good living, but also helping move technology forward in our nation.

We also hope to help students build skills for vocational work, such as crafts, fashion and design. We want to train students in other aspects of the arts and entertainment world as well, such as cosmetology. Cosmetology is a broad field, and one that is underrepresented in this part of the world. I first learned of the need for this field when we were working on the *Queen of Katwe* movie—where we had to outsource people from the U.K. and Australia to deal with this particular department.

My hope is that the learners we have already trained will be the trainers of the next generation of learners, who will train up the next generation and so on. We also hope to empower students in the realm of entrepreneurship.

We have already begun the process of building the foundation for a school, but there is still much more to do. We are operating in different regions of Uganda in partnership with various companies, schools, supporting NGOs and foundations, launching chess programs and starting to empower students.

My ultimate dream is to have a school or group of schools that encompasses all that I have laid out in one setting, to create an ideal environment for the young people of Uganda, and for those in other impoverished nations. I don't know exactly how we will make this happen yet, when it will come to fruition, or where we will ultimately end up... but I'm excited about where we are heading.

CPSIA information can be obtained
at www.ICGtesting.com
Printed in the USA
BVHW072114151019
561195BV00007B/13/P